WHEN CHILDREN PRAY

CHERI FULLER

When Children Pray

HOW GOD USES THE PRAYERS OF A CHILD

Multnomah Publishers *Sisters, Oregon*

WHEN CHILDREN PRAY
published by Multnomah Publishers, Inc.

Copyright © 1998 by Cheri Fuller
International Standard Book Number: 1-57673-288-6

Published in association with the literary agency of
Alive Communications, Inc.
1465 Kelly Johnson Blvd., Suite 320
Colorado Springs, CO 80920

Design by Kirk DouPonce
Cover photo of child by Tamara Reynolds Photography

Most Scripture quotations are from
The Holy Bible, New International Version
© 1973, 1984 by International Bible Society,
used by permission of Zondervan Publishing House.
Also quoted:
New American Standard Bible (NASB)
© 1960, 1977 by the Lockman Foundation.
The Holy Bible, King James Version (KJV)
The Amplified Bible (AMP)
© 1965 by Zondervan Publishing House.
The Living Bible (TLB)
© 1971. Used by permission of Tyndale House Publishers, Inc.
All rights reserved.
Holy Bible, New Living Translation (NLT)
© 1996. Used by permission of Tyndale House Publishers, Inc.
All rights reserved.
The New Testament in Modern English, Revised Edition (Phillips)
© 1972 by J. B. Phillips
The Message
©1993 by Eugene H. Peterson.

Printed in the United States of America
ALL RIGHTS RESERVED

For information:
MULTNOMAH PUBLISHERS, INC. • POST OFFICE BOX 1720 • SISTERS, OREGON 97759

Library of Congress Cataloging-in-Publication Data:
Fuller, Cheri
    When children pray : how God uses the prayers of a child / Cheri Fuller.
        p.   cm.
    Includes bibliographical references.
    ISBN 1-57673-288-6 (alk. paper)
    1. Prayer—Christianity. 2. Children—Religious life. 3. Parenting—Religious
aspects—Christianity. I. Title.
    BV220.F   1998   98-28069
    248.3'2'083—dc21   CIP

98 99 00 01 02 03 04 05 — 10 9 8 7 6 5 4 3 2 1

For

Caitlin Elizabeth Fuller

my precious first grandchild,

courageous and much-loved,

part of this marvelous generation

of children that I believe

God will use to change the world.

"For I know the plans that I have for you,"
declares the LORD, "Plans for welfare
and not for calamity, to give you a future and a hope."
Jeremiah 29:11 (NASB)

ACKNOWLEDGMENTS

Many thanks to the children who wrote and shared their prayers, and to the parents who told me their stories of tender moments talking to God with their kids and of prayers spoken and answered. You and your children have inspired and encouraged me! Thanks to the children of our congregation, Bridgeway Church in Oklahoma City, for allowing me the joy of praying with and learning from you as we journey to know God better.

I appreciate the awesome children's and youth leaders who shared ideas and stories, especially Jane Mackie, Jill Harris, Wayne Douglas, Pete Hohmann, Art Murphy, Dianne DuBose, Joyce Satter, Shirley Lancelot, Fawn Parish, Doug Clark, Mike Higgs, Steve Eubanks, Beth Thomas, Jan Merritt, Jerry Lenz, and Sara Parnell. Thanks also to Phama Woodyard, Melissa King, Julie Brown, and Melanie Hemry for reading the manuscript in its formative stage.

Special thanks to Fern Nichols of Moms In Touch International for being obedient to God in inspiring me and leading moms in the United States and around the world to pray for our children and their schools.

I also am thankful for Barbara James of the World Intercessors Network, both for the burden she has carried to pray for children of many nations and the inspiration and encouragement she gave me concerning this book.

Many thanks to:

My terrific agent, Greg Johnson, at Alive Communications, Inc.;

My editor, Judith Couchman, for her editorial skills, prayers, and creative insight;

The entire staff at Multnomah Publishers who have partnered with me in this project—editorial, design, marketing, publicity, and sales folks. Working with all of you is a joy;

And most of all, I thank God for my husband, Holmes, who continues to support me in all the writing and speaking endeavors God calls me to do—for his prayers, practical help, and the many unseen ways he encouraged me in this project and in our adventure of faith together.

CONTENTS

Kids at Work!

H ave you ever had an idea for a project or program that sounded great, so you took it to God and asked Him to bless it? I sure have. Maybe, like me, you've found that sometimes He graciously blesses the plan and other times you strive and strain, trying to accomplish it in your own strength.

But what a difference it makes when we recognize what God is already doing, plug into *His* plan, and pour our energies into those ideas and strategies. That's one of the reasons I'm so excited about children and prayer. I believe this topic isn't my idea or anyone else's—it's God's sovereign plan to draw kids' hearts to Himself through prayer, evidenced by the growth of a life-changing prayer movement around the world.

In the book *When Mothers Pray,* I shared my experiences and those of many moms and grandmothers who prayed for children and teenagers. I told how we, the pray-ers, were transformed; how schools and campuses were changed; how God ignited passion for Him in our kids; and how, with persevering prayer, even prodigals came home to Christ.

While I was writing that book and since its publication, one cause-and-effect fact kept emerging: When we pray for our children, earnestly seeking God on their behalf, they become pray-ers too! Over and over I saw the truth of author E. M. Bounds' observation that "Praying Samuels come from praying Hannahs."[1]

As I talked to mothers in the United States and around the world, I heard about marvelous acts of God resulting not just through the prayers of adult intercessors, but through children and youth— teenagers meeting at their campus flagpoles to pray for their classmates and schools; students praying in thousands of new high school prayer groups; children attending global prayer conferences; kids taking on-site prayer walks to intercede for legislators, neighbors, and even prisoners.

I was filled with surprise, delight, and awe as I heard about an eight-year-old girl in Santiago, Chile, who experienced God's presence so greatly that when she lay her hands on other children and prayed for them, a wave of salvation and revival touched an entire community; a nine-year-old girl whose intercession for Mongolia helped ignite spiritual awakening in that country; a group of four hundred children in a Texas church who faithfully prayed through their minister's battle with cancer; and the many kids you'll read about in this book who prayed for parents, friends, missionaries, government leaders, grandpas, and even their cats.

As I investigated what God is doing among children and youth, a window of understanding opened to my mind and light flooded in, bringing with it wonderful stories and testimonies of what happens when kids pray. I sensed that God wants children to join the wave of prayer moving through the world today. As adults pray for and support them, these kids are rising up as intercessors for their generation.

In the pages ahead you'll read stories about children who are answering God's call to prayer. You'll discover the influence parents can have, how children's youth leaders are equipping kids, and how groups of young intercessors are forming global networks to link many of these prayer teams. In the process, you'll consider how to support and equip your own children for prayer and help them develop a loving relationship with God that will last for a lifetime.

And because prayer begins in the home, you'll find practical ideas and tips about encouraging your children's spiritual lives. You'll explore advice about:

- mentoring and modeling effective prayer
- leading your children from their natural wonder to worship
- integrating prayer in your everyday family lifestyle, in natural, fun ways—no matter how busy you are
- guiding kids to compassionate servant prayers instead of just "me-centered" requests
- leading a few children or a large group to step into God's presence in intercession and hear what He wants them to pray about
- motivating kids with different bents and interests to get excited about prayer adventures and develop the confidence to pray any-time, anywhere

This book will help moms and dads guide their children in know-ing, loving, and communicating with God through prayer. But *When Children Pray* is also for Sunday school teachers, children's ministers, and Christian school teachers—anyone who wants to help kids learn to pray. In addition, you can read the book's stories to children to help them discover what happens when kids pray and inspire their own prayer lives.

When we invite, equip, and release children to pray, God's Spirit meets them and wonderful things happen. As you lead them, learn from them and observe the results, your prayer relationship with God will deepen too.

So as you read these pages, ask God to reveal how you can plug into what He's already orchestrating among children and youth through prayer. Integrate the suggestions that best work for you and your children, then hang on for an adventurous ride!

Cheri Fuller

PART ONE

What Happens When Kids Pray

Let the little children come to me!

Never send them away!

For the Kingdom of God belongs to men who have hearts

as trusting as these little children's.

And anyone who doesn't have their kind of faith

will never get within the Kingdom's gates.

JESUS CHRIST
Luke 18:16-17 (TLB)

Dear Heavenly Fafer,
Thank You for this food. Help us to feel bevver. We love You this day.

—Claire, 3

god
please show the people of this world your love give them your grace and mercy so that they will be able to minister throughout the world alos. give everyone a home. food clothing and a job.

—Aaron, 14

Dear Jesus,
Please heal my mommie. She has the cold all the way down to her heart.

—Carrie, 4

CHAPTER ONE

The Power of Youthful Prayers

Though her voice is small and mild,
All heaven stills for the prayer of a child.

AUTHOR UNKNOWN

In a small motel room in western Oklahoma, Dave bent over his laptop, booting it up to test the communications time-keeping system he planned to install for a company the next morning. To ready the equipment for installation, he needed to double-check the functions and then program the system on his computer.

ERROR, the message flashed on the screen. Then the read-out went dead.

How can this be? he thought. The system had been tested and certified by technicians. Dave tried several more functions and the error message appeared again. For hours he worked on the system, trying to detect and solve the problem. He attempted to contact technical support people in several locations but no one was available. The system had clearly failed.

Dave finally called his boss in Oklahoma City to report the status, but instead of offering him support, his boss, Dan, barraged him with an angry tirade. It wasn't like Dan to blame Dave for a technical problem like this. Besides, Dave had done everything possible, and nothing was working.

Normally quick to ask for God's guidance, Dave felt so discouraged that he couldn't pray. A heaviness descended on his mind. *I prayed earlier and it didn't help,* he thought. *And what will I tell Joel?*

Dave had brought his ten-year-old son Joel on this business trip so they could spend some quality time together, especially on the long drive to and from the company. But now things had spiraled downhill and Dave felt totally frustrated. So much for quality time.

Later when Joel returned to the room after playing Ping-Pong with another kid, he saw his dad pacing in front of the bed, visibly shaken and stressed. Dave made another phone call attempting to get technical help, then tried the computer again. Nothing. Finally he sat on the bed, head in his hands.

"What's the matter, Dad?" Joel ventured, and Dave spilled out the problem.

"Joel, this is unbelievable! There's something more at work here. I don't know what else to do because everything's gone wrong," Dave said. "Would you pray for me?"

As Joel sat on the motel bed he put one hand on his dad's shoulder and prayed, "Lord, help my dad remember how to get the time clock working and the problem solved. Help his boss to be nicer to him and not so mad. And please, take off all the pressure."

As Joel prayed, some Bible verses he'd never memorized came to his mind. He and his dad looked up the passages and read Ephesians 6:10–15, which describes our need to wear the armor of God in spiritual battle against unseen forces that muddle our thoughts and actions. Then they looked up Psalm 22:8 (NASB): "Commit yourself to the LORD; let Him deliver him. Let Him rescue him, because He delights in him."

Moved by Joel's spiritual sensitivity, Dave encouraged his son to pray each verse over him and the situation. As the boy continued to intercede, he envisioned his dad kneeling like a child, with his hands folded and head bowed. He saw Jesus kneeling beside Dave, with His hand on his father's shoulder, comforting him. As with the Scriptures, Joel shared the picture with his dad. In turn, Dave told his son how this helped him feel assured of God's help.

Although nothing about the problem changed immediately, Dave felt a heaviness lift from his spirit. He put the computer aside, believing the Lord would do what his son had prayed, and went out to play catch and enjoy the evening with him.

The next morning Dave started over and immediately discovered the source of the problem. The technical support people returned his call, and by that afternoon he had everything installed and functioning perfectly. Dan even called back to affirm Dave's hard work.

The turnaround relieved a huge stress for this dad. But the prayer time had an even more important, long-lasting impact on the ten-year-old son. Usually quiet, tentative, and not likely to take risks, Joel's faith grew swiftly and he trusted God much more in his everyday life. Before that day, fear had always been a big mountain for Joel; he often became overwhelmed and worried about a problem that erupted at school or at home. But after seeing how God answered his prayers for his dad, Joel began going to the Lord first in difficult times. He found His strength to handle problems, whether it was for writing a book report or resolving a misunderstanding with a friend.

"Jesus was right there with us in the motel," says Joel. Now he knows first-hand the truth of Psalm 22:8, that if he commits himself to the Lord, He will deliver and rescue him, just as He helped his dad that day in the motel.

And Joel's dad understands that with prayer even, "a little child shall lead them" (Isaiah 11:6).

A WIND IN SOUTH AFRICA

It was a cold, sunny, still winter's day in South Africa. A large white tent stood outside the Dutch Reformed Church at Centurion, Pretoria, where pastors, intercessory leaders, and ministry directors from around the world gathered in the main building for the 1997 Global Consultation on World Evangelization. Jane Mackie of Australia served as the intercession leader for the children at the conference, but because she also needed to attend the adult consultations, she handed leadership of the children's prayer sessions to her seventeen-year-old daughter, Ellen, and her team.

In the children's tent Ellen and the team of teenagers guided the one hundred South African children, ages five through sixteen, through the basic steps in preparation for prayer and intercession: a relationship check with God and each other; praise and worship; submitting their minds to God and inviting the Holy Spirit's presence and direction;

waiting on God for what He wanted them to pray. Toward the end of the hour, as the children shared their thoughts about what God seemed to be telling them, one girl began sobbing and a few others turned tearful.

"What's wrong? What are you upset about?" Ellen asked. The children were troubled by the violence and crime in South Africa. They felt convicted that they had grown so accustomed to it, they hardly mentioned the devastating problem in their prayers. Suddenly a line of children trailed up front to the microphone, saying things like, "We must pray for our country and not just let the older people pray. God wants us to take responsibility to pray about the violence, not just leave it to our parents to intercede."

At this point Jane dropped by the tent with a group of adult intercessors to join the children in prayer, but one of the directors said it was time to wind things up for morning tea time.

"We have one more thing the Lord wants us to do," Ellen announced. She suggested that the children pray on their knees, Korean-style (all at once), for their country. The children dropped to their knees. At the count of three they cried out to God on behalf of children, families, and others hurt by the crime and violence, and asked God to stop the destruction plaguing South Africa.

Only seconds passed before the tent began to shake; a gust of wind blew into the tent and dust flew everywhere. The children wondered what was happening, but Jane encouraged them to keep praying. As adults from the conference looked into the children's tent, they saw clusters of young people weeping and interceding for their country. After the prayer time one girl told the leadership team that when the wind was blowing, she had looked outside the tent and the trees were standing still.

"What a wonderful work they were doing in prayer," Jane recalled. She believes the Holy Spirit swept through that tent. "Only God knows the true value of the weight of those children's tears, as He collected them and used them for His purposes." [1]

At a conference of informed, experienced, adult intercessors, children led the way.

GOD'S CALL TO KIDS

Jesus said, "Let the little children come to me, and do not hinder them, for the kingdom of God belongs to such as these" (Luke 18:16). God has always welcomed children and young people into His presence, wanting them to develop a vital, prayerful communication they can maintain throughout their lives. But I believe He also is calling kids to pray at this particular time in history for two important reasons.

The first reason for God's call is in response to the onslaught of destruction aimed against this generation of children and youth. Kids today aren't just "at-risk." They're under the spiritual enemy's fire. In the last ten years more children have died in global battles than soldiers.[2] Around the world millions of children suffer and die from war, HIV/AIDS, child prostitution, and forced child labor, facing unprotected and poverty-stricken lives on the streets.[3] According to Phyllis Kilbourn, a missionary and children's advocate serving under World Evangelization for Christ International, "Millions more are beaten, battered, kidnapped, sexually abused and devalued in innumerable ways by individuals in their homes and communities."[4]

Since 1974 more than twenty million babies in the United States have died through intentionally aborted pregnancies, with 1.5 million new abortions occurring each year.[5] Children also bear the damaging brunt of a divorce rate of nearly 60 percent.[6] Violence attacks our youth. Every day over 135,000 kids carry guns and weapons to school and sometimes they open fire and kill innocent classmates. The average age of first-time drug use is thirteen years old and getting younger.[7] Satan is hard at work, trying to destroy our kids, both morally and physically.

However, this is not the first time the devil has tried to obliterate children. In the Old Testament the pharaoh's men killed Israelite baby boys at the time of Moses' birth (Exodus 1:22). Herod ordered the murder of all male children two years old and under, trying to destroy the baby Messiah Jesus (Matthew 2:16). Any time God has a special purpose for children, the enemy seems to unleash a wave of destruction on that generation. But as always, he cannot thwart God's agenda, and that plan encompasses the second reason God is calling kids to pray.

I believe God is inviting children and youth to claim their "rightful place" as intercessors for God's kingdom, no matter their age or background. David Barrett, a missiologist, estimates that 170 million Christians pray each day for revival and evangelism, and that 20 million claim prayer is their major calling. David Bryant, chairman of America's National Prayer Committee, explains: "Ten million prayer groups make revival prayer one of their primary agendas, while hundreds of prayer networks are committed to mobilizing such prayer within denominations, within cities, and within whole nations."[8]

An unprecedented river of prayer runs through America. Various tributaries flow into it, including denominational prayer focuses and organizations like Promise Keepers for men and Moms In Touch International, comprised of mothers who pray for their children and schools. There are city-wide, state-wide, and national Concerts of Prayer, multi-denominational gatherings that mobilize prayer for revival. Campaigns like A.D. 2000, the National Day of Prayer, PrayUSA!, and Campus Crusade for Christ's Forty Days of Prayer and Fasting are uniting millions to pray for revival in our nation. But the river extends far past American borders. Prayer summits and conferences in countries such as Korea, Brazil, Germany, Norway, and Taiwan are gathering thousands to pray for the advancement of Christ's kingdom.[9]

Bryant adds: "We are standing in the vortex of what may be the most significant prayer movement in the history of the church," which can lead to a worldwide spiritual awakening to Christ.[10] As God calls people of every denomination, race, and nation to this prayer movement, He is not leaving out the children! He's calling them to be a "feeder stream" in the river of prayer because they are a significant part of the Body of Christ and possess qualities that make them effective prayer warriors.

With simple, refreshing, childlike faith, many children are responding to God's call. In homes and churches, prayer gatherings and camps, kids are drawing near to the throne of grace. And it's not just young children who participate. In growing numbers teens are praying and fasting for their schools, families, and nations.

On the other hand, some of the pray-ers are very young. For example, at Calvary Chapel Christian School in Australia, a group of preschoolers and elementary-aged children took the initiative to give up their lunch break to pray every Tuesday. On different occasions, two little girls cried when praying for their fathers. One of those dads, who would have nothing to do with the church, began attending a Christian men's breakfast and later a spiritual retreat. As these children see God answer prayers for families and classmates, their faith grows stronger.

In contrast, on a global scale, children aged six to fifteen years from eight different countries attended the Global Consultation on World Evangelization (GCOWE) in Seoul, Korea, as praying delegates. GCOWE was attended by 4,500 world church leaders and thirty-eight young intercessors. These children didn't just pray for their own needs or countries, but for the children and youth of other nations.

When the A.D. 2000 prayer strategies were organized, Esther Ilnisky, founder of an international prayer network, asked, "What about the children? Who is mobilizing the children to pray?" In response, C. Peter Wagner, Fuller Theological Seminary professor and coordinator of A.D. 2000, invited Esther to select children to attend the 1995 world conference. The young people who attended GCOWE had their own prayer meetings, but they also participated in hands-on practice, praying for national leaders and problems.

"When the members of the International Children's Prayer Track drop to their knees, God shows up, bringing healing and hope," commented an adult GCOWE participant. They were the first of many children and teens who later joined in prayer gatherings and conferences around the world, sometimes with adults and sometimes meeting in local kids' prayer groups.

WHAT HAPPENS WHEN KIDS PRAY

What happens when children pray? God moves! He moves in their personal lives, as Joel and his dad experienced in the motel. Other times, He performs the extraordinary. For example, young pray-ers at GCOWE prayed about the Ebola virus that had just broken out in Africa. During the conference they prayed more than eight hours, asking God to stop the deadly virus. When, only a few days later, television and newspapers reported that the Ebola virus had suddenly stopped in its tracks,[11] the children knew their prayers had made a difference.

On another occasion when a group of Youth With a Mission "King's Kids" children took a prayer walk (in which they pray on location at a specific site in their community) to the state capitol of Oregon, they stood in the huge rotunda and asked God what was on His heart for them to pray. One of the older kids looked up and commented on how the "gold man" statue, a huge golden figure of a man on top of the rotunda, was the highest point they could see. Joyce Satter, their leader, pointed out that church steeples used to be the highest architectural structure in the city. The children were struck by the fact that now the "gold man" stood higher than places of worship. Applying that observation to their state government's spiritual condition, they prayed that God would remove any politicians serving their own selfish motives, that if anything exalted itself above God, it would be torn down.

Three days later an earthquake damaged the capital rotunda and cracked and moved the "gold man" statue. Due to the shaking, the rotunda closed for repairs for three to four years and the "gold man" was temporarily removed.[13] The young people believed God had moved in response to their prayers and were encouraged to pray even more fervently for Him to reign over all the political affairs of their state government.

These are just a few of thousands of remarkable stories about children who pray, in simple faith, for God to move in their culture. What about your kids? They may be inexperienced or disinterested in prayer. Can they become intercessors for God's kingdom?

The answer is yes! Though God responds to children's prayer groups and large gatherings, He also listens to and answers the simplest request of a single child. In fact, the river of prayer grows one person, one child, at a time, as he or she learns to pray for the people and situations of everyday life. Children learn to pray as they watch you pray, as they see you interceding on behalf of others and trusting God for the results. They learn to pray as you pray with them over their concerns, as you help them intercede for their family, their friends, their country, their world. They learn to pray as you teach them, through your own example, to go to God in praise and in need, trusting the heavenly Father with every aspect of your life.

Still, you may feel you can't get your children to sit still for their brief nightly prayers, much less join a global prayer effort. Or maybe you're weary. With your hectic schedule, it's difficult to find time and space to pray with your kids, particularly when you don't see them grow or change. Yet, with God, all things are possible—especially with prayer. By starting small and allowing the prayer times and places to grow, you can integrate prayer and intercession into your daily family life, no matter how busy you are. Eventually, at school, in church, or prayer groups and conferences, you and your kids can join the river of prayer that's flowing in small prayer closets, around family dinner tables, in churches, and big gatherings all over the world.

It begins with understanding the exceptional qualities that children bring to prayer.

A Prayer for Vision

Lord, thank You for the precious children and teens
You've entrusted to my care.
I pray you will draw them close
and give them a passion to love You and serve You.
Give me a vision of what You want to do
in the prayer lives of children,
and wisdom to know my part in Your plan.
In Jesus' name, Amen.

HELPING KIDS PRAY

As you think about teaching your kids to pray, consider the following questions:

- How would you describe the present prayer lives of your children?
- Describe what you would like your children's prayer lives to be like one year from now.
- What are you presently doing to encourage your children in prayer? What would you like to do better?
- What changes would you like to make in your own prayer life that could have a positive influence on your children?
- Is there one thing you could begin doing this week to help your children grow in their relationship with God? What is it? How will you begin?

Lord,

I just want to pray that you bless me and keep my attitude straight. I don't want to have any outbursts of anger. I don't want to disturb anyone's day. I pray that you'll bless people who want to know you and that you will run into them when they say, "I want you, Lord!"

—*Paul, 9*

dear lord,

i pray that you would help our family to be a witness to our new neighbors. in jesus' name i pray, amen

—*Hannah, 12*

Dear God,

I thank you for all you have done for me. You are swell, you are Awesome, you are Wonderful!

—*Joel, 8*

CHAPTER TWO

The Miracle of Childlike Faith

The Lord took the children in his arms,
put his hands on them and blessed them.
He never did take anybody else up in his arms like that!

J. VERNON McGEE

Chuck Pierce faced a big challenge. As a full-time ministry leader, he was helping to develop a project called the World Prayer Center. His current assignment was to lead the intercession needed for the center's fund-raising efforts. But the more Chuck prayed, the more he realized he needed "bigger faith" to fulfill his part of the project. He specifically asked God to increase his faith.

As Chuck prepared to leave on a ministry trip, his fifteen-year-old son Daniel came to him and said, "Daddy, when you're in south Texas, I believe God wants you to bring me back a parrot."

"Daniel, parrots cost a thousand dollars," Chuck replied with a laugh. "Why don't you go ask the Lord if He really wants you to have a parrot? If He does, He'll get one for you."

Accepting his dad's response, Daniel headed out of the room. About ten minutes later he returned and firmly stated, "Dad, I asked the Lord about my parrot and He said He does want me to have one."

I can't believe it. What can I say now? Chuck thought. He left for the airport, wondering if he'd somehow taught his son to try to manipulate God to get what he wanted.

When Chuck arrived in south Texas, he told his host about the conversation with Daniel. The man and Chuck had a big laugh over it but the wife looked at him and said, "Parrots fly over the border from Mexico all the time."

We could never catch a wild parrot, Chuck thought.

The next morning Chuck got up at 5 A.M. for his quiet time with God. In the middle of his devotions, he heard something outside and went to look out his window. To his surprise, he saw that the woman had set up a cage in a tree. But more surprising, she was on her knees at the base of the tree, praying.

Oh no, I've led this woman into total delusion, Chuck thought. *Does she expect a wild parrot to just walk into the cage?* Chuckling, he went back to his devotions, and later that morning led a big prayer meeting at a local church.

The next morning Chuck got up again for his quiet time and prayer for the World Prayer Center. Again, he heard something outside. He opened his window and looked outside to see the woman shutting the cage's door. A large, beautiful parrot had flown into the yard, landed on a tree limb, and walked into the waiting cage!

God then spoke to Chuck's heart: If you will have faith as a child, I will release *what you need in this season.*[1]

What is this childlike faith and why is it important in prayer?

Throughout His earthly ministry, Jesus said a lot about faith. When people showed faith, He released His power, like the centurion who said, "Just say the word, and my servant will be healed" (Matthew 8:8, NASB) and the woman who suffered from a hemorrhage and found healing when she touched the hem of Jesus' robe. "Daughter, take courage; your faith has made you well," He assured her (Matthew 9:22, NASB). When Jesus healed the blind man who cried out, He said, "Be it done to you according to your faith" (Matthew 9:29, NASB).

He also rebuked people when they lacked faith. To the disciples He asked, "You of little faith, why are you so afraid?" (Matthew 8:26) when they panicked in a storm.

Childlike faith is an "all things are possible" kind of trust in God's ability and power. Most likely it was one of the qualities Jesus referred to when He said, "Unless you are converted and become like little children, you shall not enter the kingdom of heaven" (Matthew 18:3, NASB). Pretty strong words! But without faith "it is impossible to please

Him," Hebrews 11:6 tells us, "for he who comes to God must believe that He is, and *that* He is a rewarder of those who seek Him."

Sure, kids can make big messes and be exasperating, frustrating, and delightful all in the same day. But because they have not yet learned the caution and cynicism that too often accompanies adulthood, most children naturally possess "big faith." I believe it is their wide-eyed wonder, openness and expectation that Jesus found so endearing, that prompted Him to say that all of us should maintain those childlike qualities in our prayer lives with Him. Since this quality is such an important key to effective prayer, let's look at some of the characteristics which constitute childlike faith.

BIG FAITH FOR BIG NEEDS

During delivery of her first baby, Chia, a children's pastor in Tulsa, Oklahoma, suffered an embryonic embolism, which means the fluid in the baby's sac entered her blood stream and clots were thrown to both of her lungs, which collapsed. This resulted in a series of three heart attacks and additional clots to Chia's brain. As she lay in the ICU in a coma many people prayed for her. The situation looked tragic and impossible, and some shook their heads in despair.

But thousands of miles away in England, where his parents were missionaries, knowing nothing of his former pastor's condition, five-year-old Joshua, told his mom, "Chia will live and not die. She will live and not die!" He refused to eat breakfast, saying he was going to fast and pray for Chia. His mother remained puzzled about his behavior until a few days later when they got word that Chia was in ICU. Continuing his prayer vigil, Joshua asked his mom to help him put his prayer on a cassette and send it to the hospital.

Joshua started his message by reading Psalm 27 and then sharing about his baby sister Jennifer, his mom and dad, and his new BMX bicycle. He concluded by saying, "I'm going to end this tape by praying for you. In the name of Jesus, I speak to those blood clots in Chia's head and I speak life to Chia and I know she will live and not die and I want her to go back to her house soon and take care of her baby girl and enjoy her…by His stripes you are healed, Chia. In the name of Jesus, I ask that the Spirit of the Lord would heal you, Chia, and help you get well. And I'll keep praying for you until I hear that you're totally, totally, fully well, and I love you, and I just want to end this tape by saying, Love from Joshua! Three kisses, three big hugs and three big prayers until you are well!"

The prayers of this five-year-old reached heaven. Chia's physician later reported in her medical records: "This is the most amazing case I've ever seen in my medical practice. For the first three or four days of this horrendous episode, the patient was considered to be essentially brain dead. She showed only minimal progress. Then she showed an apparent miraculous recovery. The medical aspects of this case are detailed in the progress notes. What is not in the notes, however, is the extreme and continued support and prayer of family and friends. This is the most amazing thing I've ever seen and must be considered a miracle."[2]

Grateful for the big faith of a young boy, Chia is alive today. After two months in the hospital and a year in therapy, she made continual progress. Her daughter is now eleven years old.

Faith came naturally to Daniel and Joshua, and it's a quality that particularly fits kids for prayer. They believe God can do anything, and that's an important part of a relationship with Him. Where does this faith come from? I love how Gloria Gaither explains it:

> Children possess an uncanny ability to cut to the core of the issue, to expose life to the bone, and strip away the barnacles that cling to the hull of our too sophisticated pseudo-civilization. One reason for this, I believe, is that children have not mastered our fine art of deception that we call "finesse." Another is that they are so "lately come from" that faith and trust are second nature to them. They have not acquired the obstructions to faith that come with education; they possess instead unrefined wisdom, a gift from God.[3]

HEARTS OF COMPASSION

Children may be small but they have enormous hearts. They feel deeply about problems and suffering in the world and can pray with compassion, another key ingredient of effective prayer. They talk to God from the heart about the pain they see and experience in the world.

Abby, an Oklahoma fifth-grader, wrote the following response to the 1995 bombing of the Murrah Federal Building in her city:

Lord, we have taken a great fall,
and You have caught us in Your gentle, loving hands.
Lord, our tears have fallen like tiny waterfalls,
and You have dried them with Your love.
Lord, we needed someone to blame—and chose You.
This was wrong, but the way You replied
was by forgiving us and comforting us even more.
Lord, there is no way of telling You
how much Your love is helping us get through this tragedy,
so we will only say this: "Thank You." [4]

A compassionate prayer from a little one can also bring healing. Ken had prayed with and for his daughter Kerry since her birth, and she grew up feeling comfortable talking with God from an early age. When she was three years old, this prayer power rescued her dad.

One weekend when Kerry visited her single dad's home, he suffered excruciating pain from a kidney infection. The doctor's office was closed, and Ken dreaded spending the money for the emergency room. Besides, who'd take care of Kerry if he had to be admitted? At his wit's end with pain, he asked her, "Kerry, Daddy really hurts—would you pray for me?"

Kerry felt sad for her daddy and wanted to help. She put her hand on his stomach and asked God to heal him, closing her simple prayer "In Jesus' name." Not long after her prayer, Ken tucked his daughter in bed for the night, retired to his own bed, and slumbered through the night for the first time in days. When he woke up, the pain was gone.

Maybe children's prayers are so effective because tenderhearted kids like Abby and Kerry connect to and represent the heart of Jesus. When Christ saw the multitudes, He was "moved with compassion for them, because they were weary and scattered, like sheep having no shepherd" (Matthew 9:36, NKJV). The Bible provides many snapshots of Christ's compassion: how He had compassion and touched those with blind eyes (Matthew 20:34), how He fed the people because of His love for them (Matthew 15:32–37), how He had mercy on a demoniac boy and restored him to sanity (Matthew 17:18). Likewise, God tells us to clothe ourselves with compassion toward others (Colossians 3:12).

Children often feel such compassion for friends and family, but they also often show compassion for people they've never met who live thousands of miles away. When Hope Smith, a nine year old, was researching a report on Mongolia as a homeschool project, one fact about that country moved her deeply. In a foreign missions magazine, Hope read that in Mongolia there were very few Bibles and that instead of worshiping God the people knelt at Buddhist altars in their tents. The fact that over 98 percent of Mongolians were spiritually lost touched Hope's heart, and she began praying.

Hope prayed that God would replace the Buddhist altars with Bibles and send more missionaries to share the gospel of Christ. But she didn't stop with a one-time prayer. Hope faithfully interceded every day for this unreached country and its people.

After two years of prayer, Hope read another article in the same magazine, this one entitled, "Hope for Mongolia." The feature story described a revival in that country, with 500 people accepting Christ as their Savior. Hope felt this was God's way of saying He had answered her prayer. During the next year those 500 Christian believers in Mongolia grew to 1,000 and the people started a church called "Hope Assembly." More than 2,000 Mongolians gathered for their first-ever Christmas service, and this church has already planted another church in Mongolia.[5]

God used the compassion and faithful prayers of a nine year old, weaving them together with the prayers of others interceding for a nation, to bring the biggest spiritual awakening in Mongolia's history. Perhaps not ironically, the first church bore Hope's name!

TRUST IN GOD'S PROVISION

We adults tend to see obstacles and analyze complications until our problems begin to look like a mountain. We ask, *How can God do anything?* Kids, on the other hand, have a wonderfully simple trust. They believe God is bigger than the mountain, that He can move anything and provide anything—even a horse.

When a California family moved from a small lot in a big city to seven country acres in Oklahoma, their children couldn't wait to learn to ride horses. They enrolled in "Pony Club," a once-a-month group where kids learned to ride and care for horses. Pony Club was great, but Dallas, the six-year-old daughter, really wanted a horse of her own. With an old farmhouse that badly needed fixing up and many other expenses, there was absolutely no money for a horse. Her parents told her to put the request in God's hands by praying about it.

At every meal and every night before she lay down to sleep, Dallas earnestly prayed for a horse. After a week of fervent prayer, she confidently announced at the breakfast table, "Dad needs to go ahead and fix the fences!"

"Why fix the fences now? We've got lots of other things we have to do first," her mom answered.

"Because our horses will get out through the holes unless they are fixed!" Dallas replied.

"But honey, God doesn't answer prayers that quickly. It takes a lot longer."

"The horses are coming. They'll be here soon. So Dad needs to fix the fences! God told me He's sending horses!" Dallas said.

Only two days later, a young woman who taught at Pony Club unexpectedly appeared at their door with two older but fine Arabian mares. If the family would take care of the horses and let them graze on their seven acres, Dallas and her siblings could ride them whenever they wanted. Dad fixed the fences so the horses wouldn't get out, and for almost two years the children got to ride the horses morning and night.

But what about when a child's desire or need is a more serious one, like the need for food? God is in the business of providing for serious needs as well, and in some cases through the prayers of a child. In 1905 the staff of an orphanage in Bethany, Oklahoma, prayed and fasted, asking God to send the money and needed supplies to care for the orphans. Like George Mueller, the faith-filled British pastor who directed orphanages without asking for donations, they spoke only to God of their need. They found victory in some areas, but the asked-for money and supplies didn't come. Rations were meager and the children were hungry.

Finally one day little Blanche, six years old, cried, "Aunt Mattie, I want bread, meat, butter, gravy, and fruit." Mattie, the orphanage director, told Blanche to ask her Father in heaven for the food, and the girl took this instruction seriously. Blanche disappeared for awhile, then emerged from her retreat, clapping her little hands and shouting, "Dory to Dod, Dory to Dod! He is going to div us the good things." In a short while a wagon drove up to the kitchen door with everything—even the exact food—the child wanted. Even the rent was paid. God was honored, and little Blanche along with Mattie and her staff, were strengthened in their faith.[6] All because a small child asked God to provide for her needs.

James tells us "Every good and perfect gift is from above, coming down from the Father of the heavenly lights" (James 1:17) and He delights to give good gifts to His children. God, our Father, who feeds the sparrows and dresses the lilies, can provide for the needy, whether big or small, as we approach Him with simple childlike faith.

STRAIGHTFORWARD SIMPLICITY

Children also tend to be simple, straightforward, and honest with God in their prayers. While adults may long-windedly hash over the problem they're praying about (as if God isn't aware of it), kids pray short, to-the-point requests. Jesus must have appreciated brevity because He warned people not to imitate those who utter long, wordy prayers. He advised, "Do not use meaningless repetition, as the Gentiles do, for they suppose that they will be heard for their many words. Therefore, do not be like them, for your Father knows what you need, before you ask Him" (Matthew 6:7–8, NASB).

I've personally experienced how a straightforward, short prayer can have a powerful effect. An eight-year-old girl prayed for me recently when I was very concerned about an issue in my life. "Jesus, show Cheri that You are right there with her, that You know what her problem is. Let her feel Your love," she said, holding my hand. As she spoke those few words, Christ's peace and presence filled me and swept away the frustration. She didn't have to know the complications of my struggle or itemize them for God. She just succinctly prayed from her heart.

And lest you worry about children carrying the burdens they pray for around with them, let me encourage you: I've observed that children seem to "let go and let God" easier than adults. They tend to drop the need at Jesus' feet when they pray, even if it's a heavy one. Fully expecting God to handle the difficulty, they run off to play only a few minutes after saying "amen." I found this out as a young mother when, after prayer, I'd continue to fret about a problem. My kids would remind me, "Mom, I thought we already prayed about that. You don't have to worry about it now." Out of the mouths of babes...

KEEPING SHORT ACCOUNTS

Kids also keep shorter accounts with God more easily than adults do. Recently I spent time with three young boys, aged four, five, and eight, and as we prepared to pray we talked about confession and forgiveness.

"Have you done anything lately that you think made God sad?" I asked them. "Why don't we ask God to show us and then talk to Him about it? Would you do that with me?"

All three little guys nodded their heads and before long, four-year-old Daniel spoke up. "I remember I was so angry at lunchtime today because I wanted to say grace by myself but everybody else got to say it too. I was so mad."

"Do you want to tell God you're sorry?" I asked.

He prayed, "Dear Jesus, I was angry today that I wanted to say grace but everyone joined in. Please wash my sin away and change my heart. In Jesus' name. Amen." He smiled as he looked up at me.

Then it was Josh's turn. "You know," he said, "I got angry at my friend today because he stole my eraser. And that was my favorite eraser! I felt like doing something to him, but I didn't." Then he prayed, "Jesus, I am sorry that I got angry today when my friend stole my eraser, please forgive me. Cleanse me and please change my heart. Amen."

When Josh finished, four-year-old Jeremy chimed in, not only asking God to forgive him for a bad attitude toward two girls in his class who'd been unkind to him, but to help him love them more. The transparency and open-heartedness of these boys humbled me and warmed my heart.

God loves it when we quickly repent and turn to Him as children do because if we harbor sin or unforgiveness in our heart, the Lord won't hear our prayers (Isaiah 59:2). But when we agree with God about our sin, we're restored to fellowship with Him and our hearts are cleansed. Like children, our hearts can stay tender as we keep short accounts with God and others.

HEARING GOD SPEAK

Children's ability to hear God is often unsullied by past experiences. They seem to have a way of knowing, of being tuned in to a divine wavelength. And if we listen to them, we can learn much—occasionally something we really need to know.

In her book *Beyond the Veil*, Alice Smith recalls the time her young son Bryan came into the kitchen for a snack and casually said, "Mom, you need to have some candles ready."

"Why do we need candles?" she asked her son.

"We are going to have a bad storm and the lights are going to go out," Bryan replied, even though outside it was a lovely, cloudless day.

"How do you know that? Did you hear something on TV?" his mom asked.

"No, I just feel the Lord has told me we're to be ready for a storm."

Alice found candles and put them out on the counter. Less than an hour later, a huge thunderstorm and tornado roared through their neighborhood. The lights flickered and went out. The next morning broken trees, tree limbs, and roofing shingles lay all over the streets. Bryan was apparently listening to God and heard Him correctly.[7] His mom was glad she'd paid attention too!

WHAT CAN WE DO?

"Who is the greatest in the kingdom of heaven?" the disciples asked Jesus. He didn't point to the top Pharisees or high-ranking army officers. Instead, He placed a small child in their midst and replied, "Truly, I say to you, unless you are converted and become like children, you shall not enter the kingdom of heaven" (Matthew 18:1, NASB). The Master wanted adults to recapture the childlike faith and trust of children. As Alan D. Wright says in *A Chance at Childhood Again,* "Children have the most of heaven because they don't see lines and limitations around themselves or around God."[8]

If children have the capability to be powerful pray-ers like Josh and Hope, to pray with great faith as Dallas and Daniel did, to feel deeply about the suffering in the world as Abby has, then we need to change our minds about kids! We need to understand God's mindset about children and explore the amazing learning and spiritual capacity they bring to prayer.

A Prayer of Blessing

Lord, You took children into Your arms,

loving and blessing them.

Help me to love and bless children as You did—

my own and those in my church, school, and neighborhood.

Help me to be more like them, in trust, compassion, and openness.

Restore in me a childlike faith and a clean heart.

Give me Your eyes to see them,

to see the potential You've put within them,

and the unique qualities each is gifted with.

In Jesus' name, Amen.

HELPING KIDS PRAY

Think about these questions today:

- What characteristics do you see in your children that "fit" them for prayer?
- How could you encourage and cultivate those qualities in their lives?
- Which of the characteristics discussed in this chapter—faith, compassion, brevity, being quick to repent and forgive, quick to hear God—have you lost in your journey to adulthood? Ask God to restore these qualities to your prayer life.

Dear God,
You are the best and full of glory, Lord. And one more thing: thank you for my baby brother. Love, Christina

—Christina, 9

dear lord
please help the sick get well like my best friend who has a birth defect and my friend's mom who has m.s. help those who don't know you draw closer to you. help missionaries around the world be comforted by your love in a land where they are the only known americans and sometimes the only known christians. like my friend in india. in jesus name. amen

—Emily, 13

Dear God,
I LUV YOU
Ben

—Ben, 8

CHAPTER THREE

Changing Our Minds about Kids

Give me the children until they are seven,
And anyone may have them afterward.

St. Francis Xavier

A few years ago Brenda Steen, a California pastor, felt led by God to start a prayer group at her church. At the next Wednesday night service, she announced the first meeting and invited anyone in the congregation to come.

The evening of the first prayer meeting, Brenda arrived early, knelt at the altar, and began to pray, waiting for others to join her. Soon she heard others praying, but the voices weren't those of adults. The sounds of children praying—first praising God, then praying for their concerns—floated through the room.

"Oh, God, you're humongous! You have tons of glory!" Christian, 9, said.

Jordan, 4, prayed fervently, "God, I claim the whole world's salvation! Not half the world, the *whole world!*"

Brenda and the few adults who had trickled into the room watched with wonder as God orchestrated the newborn prayer group. Five years later, the weekly group is still going strong, and at times the kids have begged Brenda to join them for an all-night prayer session.

Many adults don't think of children as powerful intercessors or understand that young ones can initiate prayer. But kids often possess a greater learning ability than we give them credit for. For example, current research in the brain development of babies and young children reveals that they have much more potential to learn in the early years than experts previously believed. Children have a greater potential for learning language (including foreign language), math, and music than we ever thought possible. Before toddlers can speak "adult" language, they can understand a hundred words or more. Preschoolers can add before they can count. Babies and preschoolers' memories are excellent. (That's why we need to watch what we say around them. Their minds function like tape recorders that soak up everything they hear!) [1]

In a similar way, children have more spiritual capacity than we imagine, especially in prayer. Those who work, play, and pray with children know there is no junior version of the Holy Spirit. The same Spirit who burdens adult Christians to pray for an unsaved person at home or for an unreached people in a foreign country also indwells Christian children. God can tell a seven-year-old what to pray, just as He reveals His will to a twenty-seven or seventy year old. In fact, children can sometimes hear God and pray simple prayers that hit the target better than adults can.

Atarah McCrae, an eight-year-old California girl, "hit the target" in prayer for her father's needs. One afternoon Atarah's father, who lived in Oregon and was remarried, called her to talk. She answered his questions and told him about school.

Then Atarah asked, "Can I pray for you, Dad?"

"Sure, if you want to," he answered.

As Atarah prayed for her dad, she asked God to bless him and touch his mind and heart:

Lord, bring angels around his home and bless his wife. Strengthen him and help him give up the things that aren't like You, God. I ask You to take away the things hurtful and harmful to him and especially take away the taste of alcohol from his mouth. Give him a mind that wants to serve and worship You. In Jesus' name, Amen.

Atarah's mom stood by and marveled. She had prayed for her ex-husband many times but she had never asked God to take away her ex-husband's taste and desire for alcohol. Although Atarah's dad had been addicted to alcohol for seven years, within the month, he was totally free of his drinking habit. Every Sunday since that time two years ago, he's attended church faithfully and his life has turned around for the better.

GOD USES CHILDREN IN HIS PLAN

Praying children aren't a new phenomenon. Throughout Scripture and history God has clearly honored children by using them to accomplish His plan. David was just a young shepherd when he defeated Goliath and saved the Israelites from the Philistines (1 Samuel 17). Both Jeremiah and Daniel were young men whom God used mightily (Jeremiah 1:4–19; Daniel 1–2). Mary was only a young adolescent when God tapped her to bear and nurture His Son (Matthew 1:18–25).

Before any of these important youth came Samuel, whose mother Hannah had given him to God before his birth. "For his whole life he will be given over to the LORD," she vowed (1 Samuel 1:28).

"[Samuel] was born of a praying mother, whose heart was full of earnest desire for a son," writes E. M. Bounds. "He came into life under prayer surroundings, and his first months in this world were spent in direct contact with a woman who knew how to pray.... It was no wonder he developed into a man of prayer."[2]

In those days evil abounded among the Israelites, particularly in the priesthood, so words and visions from God were almost nonexistent. Eli the priest had grown old, and through the years he hadn't restrained his sons Hophni and Phineas, who had defiled the sacrifices in the temple. The sons sinned blatantly against God and abused His people; when Eli attempted some belated correction they only ignored him. So God pursued another plan for ministering to His people. He promised, "I will raise up for myself a faithful priest, who will do according to what is in my heart and mind. I will firmly establish his house, and he will minister before my anointed one always" (1 Samuel 2:35).

Was that faithful priest a man who had apprenticed in the temple and studied for years? No, the priest was little Samuel, Hannah's boy, whose name meant "asked of God." Samuel grew into a man of prayer and served as God's vessel to bring about His purpose during a specific time in Israel's history. Throughout his lifetime Samuel turned to God in prayer.

When the people fell into idolatry and the Ark of God was taken by their enemies, Samuel beseeched them to turn back to the Lord. But he also prayed: "Assemble all Israel at Mizpeh and I will intercede with the LORD for you" (1 Samuel 7:5). In other crises later in Samuel's life, such as when the Israelites demanded a king or when Saul disobeyed God's divine instructions for battle against the Amalekites, Samuel was grieved and prayed to the Lord on behalf of the sinful people (1 Samuel 8:6; 15:11).

Still, the first time young Samuel was called by God, he didn't recognize the Lord's voice in the night. Assuming that Eli had called him, Samuel climbed out of bed and walked to the old man's room. Eventually Eli discerned that God was calling the boy and instructed him to return to bed and lie down. He also told Samuel to say, "Speak, LORD, for your servant is listening," when the Lord called again.

The ensuing words from God must have been difficult for a young child to hear and deliver! Eli instructed Samuel to speak honestly and exactly what he'd heard God say, no matter what the message. And even though the words of judgment meant death for Eli and his sons, the old priest taught the boy how to hear God and speak His truth.

Somehow Eli realized that Samuel's spiritual capacity was greater than his age or size. Consequently, Samuel grew both as a priest and an intercessor, and God "let none of his words fall to the ground" (1 Samuel 3:19). Though Eli wasn't an effective father, he did mentor Samuel with guidance in responding to God, which helped the young man learn to hear God and speak His message.

Besides Scripture, there are other historical accounts that describe how God has used young people, especially in revival. John Wesley, the renowned Methodist preacher, wrote in his journals about children as young as preschoolers who not only rejoiced in God's grace but also prayed powerfully for others. Wesley often preached to children and had a great desire for the "head knowledge" of Christ to move into their hearts so they could powerfully experience God's love.

"I was awaked between four and five, by the children vehemently crying to God," wrote Wesley about the young ones sleeping in rooms nearby. "The maids went to them at five. And first one of the boys, then another, then one and another of the maids, earnestly poured out their souls before God, both for themselves and for the rest. They continued weeping and praying till nine o'clock, not thinking about meat or drink...but remained in words or groans calling upon God."[3]

He wrote about the English children of Kingswood: "I examined sixteen of them, who desired to partake of the Lord's Supper. Nine or ten had a clear sense of the pardoning love of God.... Eighteen of the children from that time met in three bands. These were remarkable for their love to each other, as well as for steady seriousness. They met every day; besides which, all the children met in class."[4] At Everton, another English town he ministered in, Wesley reported, "Yea, many children here have had far deeper experience, and more constant fellowship with God, than the oldest man or woman at Everton."[5]

Years later, between 1949 and 1952, a wave of revival moved over the Hebrides Islands off the coast of Scotland. Spiritual life in the town of Berneray had been bleak and barren. Some of the Christian men in the village asked a seventeen-year-old boy, Donald Smith, to join them for a church meeting because of his reputation for effective prayer. Asked to lead the prayer, Donald stood and poured his heart out to his "covenant-keeping God."

Almost instantly the Spirit swept into the group gathered in that church and touched its members with convicting power. Simultaneously, people in the village, touched by God's Spirit, repented of their sins and turned to Christ. Shortly thereafter, the roads were filled with people streaming from every direction to the church.[6]

When adults realize children's potential for prayer and mentor them to enter into God's presence, pray, and listen to His voice, kids can change destiny. God wants to use our young ones now, just as He did in biblical times and in history.

CHANGING OUR LIMITED VISION

For years, and with good intentions, I taught Sunday School by creating activities, telling flannelgraph stories, asking children to fill in sheets about Bible characters or the fruit of the Spirit, and helping them learn the books of the Bible. These were good projects that kept children busy, but I missed out on God's desire to profoundly touch children and their world through prayer. In recent years God has been broadening my vision, showing me how to lead kids on prayer adventures instead of just keeping them occupied while their parents tend to "real" spiritual matters in adult services.

One of those times was a Sunday morning prayer walk, when a few adults accompanied a group of children who prayed as they strolled around the public elementary school near the church. In my small group one girl saw the blue "Disabled Parking" sign and remembered the students with learning and physical handicaps who attended the school.

"Let's pray for them," Mary said, and she did: "Jesus, help the children who have trouble learning and who have to be in wheelchairs or are handicapped. Protect them from teasing and let them know You love them."

A few minutes later as we continued around the building, Jenny piped up with a comment. "I was really sad when my parents got a divorce," she said. "Let's pray for those kids whose moms and dads are divorced."

"Help their parents to be godly and loving," she prayed. "Help their families get back together and please comfort the kids, Jesus."

The children prayed for teachers to know God, for the principal's heart to be soft and not mean, for every student to be saved, and even for the janitor. Our prayer walk took only twenty minutes, but I believe it made an eternal difference.

Maybe like me, you've thought kids have short attention spans. We think they can't pray very long and we have to keep them busy. Actually, I've found they can pray effectively when we tailor prayer times to their present ability to focus and show them how to target their prayers.

Or maybe you've thought, *When my kids grow up and commit to serve God, go to Bible college or seminary, then He can use them.* On the contrary, God wants to use them now! God *is* using children and youth. They can affect the spiritual kingdom *now, not later;* there's so much more for them to do than simply be entertained. God loves and desires the prayers of children and there are so many prayers He wants them to pray.

CULTIVATE A RELATIONSHIP WITH GOD

So how can we begin changing our minds about the spiritual capacity of our kids?

First, we must cultivate our children's relationship with God, believing that they're capable of loving, relating to, and obeying Him with sensitivity and depth. As I talk with moms, dads, and grandmothers at seminars and conferences, I hear their desires for spiritually alive children:

"I want my children to love God."

"I want my sons *to want* to go to church and youth group."

"I don't want my kids to go down the drain spiritually like I see happening to lots of young people. How can I raise my children to live close to God and choose His way?"

One guideline: Start young. Teach them to talk to God when they're toddlers. Pray with them throughout childhood. Capturing children's hearts for prayer now increases the likelihood of their becoming pray-ers for a lifetime, especially through the potentially turbulent teen years. We can't change their hearts; only God can. But we can take advantage of the years when childlike faith (instead of cynicism) fills kids' hearts. We can model how to share thoughts with God in a natural, unself-conscious manner. If we disciple them in prayer, they will learn to communicate and build a personal relationship with God.

In *You Can Change the World,* author Jill Johnstone explains, "Prayer is simply talking with God. As we do this, we get to know Him better, to understand His ways, to love Him, and become His friends. When we pray we work together with God—and He wants to change the world!"[7] Through the prayer process, children connect to the Lord in their early years and develop in that relationship, loving Him more as they grow taller and older. They can experience answers to prayer and build their own history of God's faithfulness, a spiritual legacy that follows them into their adolescent and adult years.

We want to guide and protect our children, but as hard as we try, we can't always "be there" in every situation to shelter them from crises and disappointments. However, when children connect to God (whose name *Jehovah-Shammah* means "The Lord My Helper")—who will never leave or forsake them, whose eye is always upon them, who is always there (Hebrews 13:5–6)—they can develop a wonderful security. They know they're not to fear or dread because the Lord is with them, and this trusting relationship grows strong in the soil of prayer.

Sometimes that knowledge, that secure relationship of child to Father, can be a lifesaver to a family. On Christmas night, Shawna, a thirteen year old, boarded a small plane with her uncle, aunt and cousin to view the holiday lights over the lake near their home in Amarillo, Texas. After only a few minutes of flight, the plane hit turbulence and the engines sputtered. Shawna's uncle immediately turned the plane around in an attempt to fly back to the airport. Instead, the engine lost all power and their plane headed straight for a canyon wall. Remarkably, he crash-landed the plane on a small piece of land inside Ransom Canyon.

When Shawna awakened after being knocked unconscious by the impact, she saw her uncle straddling a cactus which held him from falling down a forty-foot ravine; her cousin lay under a wing of the plane; her aunt lay in puddles of gasoline with both legs broken.

Stunned and unsure of their location, Shawna pulled herself out of the plane. In the dark, the only things she could see were lights moving in the distance. *Maybe that's the highway,* Shawna thought. *If only I could get up to the highway, I could get help.*

"I love you. I'm going to get you help," she told her uncle, and took off walking. When she reached the rocks, she tried to climb up and out of the canyon, but with every attempt her already cut and bruised body slid back down the rocks.

"Finally I'd fallen so many times, I couldn't move," says Shawna. "But I knew that if I didn't get help, my aunt and uncle would die. I sat on the canyon floor and prayed simply, 'God, I can't do this without You. I don't have the strength to do this. Would You give me the strength to make it to the top?'"

Trusting His help, she took one more step and suddenly stood on the pavement of the highway. Shawna stumbled in the direction of the lights. The second car to appear stopped, and the driver drove her to the nearest ambulance service where a medical team rushed her to a hospital and dispatched helicopters to rescue her relatives.

Now eighteen years old, Shawna still believes angels carried her that mile straight up the canyon, over the barbed wire fences and huge boulders, to get help for her family.

BECOME PARTNERS IN PRAYER

Second, to change our minds about kids we can ask them to partner with us in prayer. Too often children are treated as "underlings" or appendages rather than viable, much-needed participants in intercession. Partnerships start at home by asking our children to participate with us in conversations with God.

Remember Dave and his son Joel in chapter 1? Praying for a malfunctioning computer system wasn't the first time Dave and his son had prayed together. Dave and his wife, Janet, wanted their children to believe that prayer is as natural as breathing—that we need to connect with God continually and that He's always listening. So they regularly involved their children in outreaches to others; prayer formed an essential element of that ministry. The couple taught their kids to pray in the context of loving others and meeting their needs. Each child had ministered with dad and mom in the inner city, helping them pray for the sick, poor, and desperate. By getting involved, their children saw that prayer connects people to God and that His power flows through ordinary people.

In many small, daily situations, Dave and Janet had shown Joel and his siblings that prayer is our number one tool for dealing with problems. He taught them that all of life is a schoolroom in which both adults and children learn life's lessons. The dad also stressed the principles of James 1:2–5:

> Consider it pure joy, my brothers, whenever you face trials of many kinds, because you know that the testing of your faith develops perseverance.... If any of you lacks wisdom, he should ask God, who gives generously to all without finding fault, and it will be given to him.

Thus, based on his previous prayer experiences, Joel trusted God in prayer for a faulty computer. Though he didn't understand complex computer functions and hadn't prepared the specific verses to share with his dad, the Holy Spirit brought them to mind as the young boy prayed. Joel prayed in partnership with his dad, and God intervened.

As we invite our children to partner with us in prayer, we'll observe how God uses their childlike faith to bless people and situations near and far.

CULTIVATE A VISION FOR THE WORLD

Third, we can change our minds about kids by helping them cultivate a vision for the world. Again, prayer starts at home with concerns about personal needs, family concerns, and circumstances with friends and school. But as children grow in prayer on the home front, they can gradually discover how to influence the world without leaving their bedrooms. When children find they can impact a country's president with their prayers, that someone can turn to Christ because they prayed, that they can help shape the world through intercession, it's exciting! They're less inclined to grow bored with Christianity, and likely to pray more.

As with adults, children and young people need something bigger than themselves to invest in. Even at a young age they long for purpose and want to make a difference. Through prayer they can partner with God, influencing much more than just family, friends, and schools. Prayer gives children a place to belong in the local and global spiritual communities; it increases their faith to pray internationally and care about people different from themselves.

One way we cultivate this vision is through daily conversations with God. As Christy, a Massachusetts mom, prays with her five-year-old son Jeremy each night, they use "My Family's Prayer Calendar."[8] Every day the calendar focuses on a different group of people or prayer topic: ministers at their church, the local school, a neighbor, a specific country. When they prayed for a sick neighbor and she recovered, when they prayed for the new church and Jeremy can now see it being built, his trust deepened. When they prayed for Africa and China, it broadened his view and helped him know God wants to work in many different people's lives.

In a similar way, as we position children as pray-ers in local churches, it will increase their vision for their church, community, country, and world. We can invite children to join in community outreaches, include them on prayer walks, and welcome them at large and small prayer gatherings and missions conferences. We can also help form small, ongoing prayer groups for children.

Several years ago while Jill Johnstone was writing *You Can Change the World,* she shared with her children's prayer club how the Albanian people, under Communist rule, were not allowed to worship God or read books about Him. It was against the law to pray and parents were forbidden to teach their own children about Jesus.

The children were grieved for the Albanians and prayed hard for change in that country. They made the country's struggle for freedom an ongoing prayer focus, and every week lifted up the Albanians in prayer. Eventually the Communist government in Albania fell from power and both Christians and Muslims could practice their religion.

"The children's prayers, and those of other Christians around the world, changed Albania," Jill writes.[9]

When we change our minds about children's capacity to pray, we can roll up our sleeves and teach them how to pray. We can unfold the awesome privilege of stepping into God's presence and help them discover the astonishing power of even one child's prayer.

A Prayer for Understanding

Lord, I admit that I've underestimated children
and often not understood Your ways and plans for them.
Open the eyes of my understanding so I can see
the children in my life as You see them.
Change my limited perspectives and
broaden my vision of their spiritual capacity.
Teach me to pray so we can lead and equip them
with what they need to enter into prayer.
In Jesus' name, Amen.

HELPING KIDS PRAY

When I talked to Atarah, the nine year old whose prayer helped transform her father's alcoholism and who has been asked to lead prayer for her community in the Ventura County National Day of Prayer gathering, I asked how she developed a desire to pray for others.

"It all started the first day I went to a prayer meeting with my mother," she replied. Shy and nervous, Atarah didn't know what to pray and asked her mom for help.

In the days and weeks following, Atarah's mother taught her the Lord's Prayer and the different names for God that reveal His character. She also showed Atarah how to pray God's Word when He brings Scripture to mind.

"And most of all, she taught me that every time I pray for someone, God will be pleased," Atarah said. "I got my inspiration from her, my stepdad, and grandma because my family loves to pray!"

Three suggestions:

- Help your child hear God. During family devotions or bedtime prayers, share with your child that the Bible tells us to "Be still, and know that I am God" (Psalm 46:10). Suggest that he or she sit for a few moments, as quiet as possible, and listen for God. Then ask, "What thoughts did you have?" Encourage your child by sharing that "God loves for you to be with Him."

- Ask your child to pray. When you face a challenge in your job or ministry, ask your child to pray for you. Then after the problem is resolved, share how God answered your child's prayers.

- Join or start a Moms In Touch prayer group that prays weekly for your children and their school. By becoming involved in a regular group focused on intercession, you will not only be covering your child with a blanket of prayer, but you will learn to pray scripturally, learn more about God's character and faithfulness, and grow in your scriptural life. Call 1-800-949-MOMS for resources or to find a local group.

PART TWO

Teach Your Children Well

Would we have praying men in our churches?

We must have praying mothers to give them birth,

praying homes to color their lives,

and praying surroundings to impress their minds

and to lay the foundations

for praying lives.

E. M. BOUNDS

Dear God,
I hope we will be safe. I'm sorry for when I bugged my brother. Love, Macy

—*Macy, 7*

dear god
thank you so much for being there when i needed you. also. i
pray that rachel's heart will get better and that you will just heal
her. love. bonnie

—*Bonnie, 10*

Dear God,
I pray for the bleeding children,
For the broken hearts.
I ask you to clean my heart.

—*Jessica, 8*

CHAPTER FOUR

Praying Parents, Praying Kids

*I'd rather see a sermon
than hear one any day;
I'd rather one should walk with me
than merely tell the way.*

EDGAR A. GUEST

One hot summer day a mom was fixing lunch for guests. Her kindergarten son popped in and out of the kitchen while playing in another room.

"Can't you stop and play with me, Mommy? Could we go to the park?" he called.

"No, son," his mom answered. "I've got six people who will be here soon to eat with us, the air conditioner broke, and there's so much to do!" As she labored over the stove, he followed her around, chatting.

When the guests were seated around the table, the mom asked her son, "Honey, would you say the blessing for us?"

"Oh, Mom, I don't know what to say," he objected.

"Just pray what you've heard me pray."

The little boy looked around the table and sighed, then folded his hands and said, "Oh, God, why did I invite these people here on a hot day like this?"

Picture another dinner table. Each night John Paul, his wife Sara, and sons Jacob, three years old, and Noah, barely a year old, held hands while John Paul led them in a prayer of thanks and blessing for their dinner. A few months later, though, John Paul had to work nights and couldn't be with his family for the evening meal.

At their first meal without John Paul, Sara asked her three year old, "Since Daddy's not here, would you pray for us, Jacob?"

Jacob took his baby brother's hand and his mother's hand and then prayed, "Father, God, we just thank You for this day and everything that You have given us. We ask that You bless this food, in Jesus' name, Amen." A tear trickled down Sara's cheek. Jacob had almost exactly prayed his dad's words from the Sunday before.

Jacob had listened to his father's prayers and used them as a model for his own. Because kids primarily learn by imitation, it's no surprise that they discover how to pray from praying parents. Parental example packs a lot of power in children's lives, whether it's teaching them to wear seatbelts, be honest, or bow in prayer. Kids are careful observers, and often what they see us do is just what they do.

PARENTS AS PRAYER MENTORS

"Once my mother sat silently in the car in the mall parking lot," remembers thirteen-year-old Emily. "When I asked her what she was doing, she told me she was praying to find the right dress for a conference because we didn't have much time. We walked in and found a dress; she tried it on and it was just right! It really helped me learn that it doesn't have to be a huge prayer. It can be small. Her example really helped me."

Emily is right. When we're prayer examples, we help our kids learn the value of going to God with the little things as well as the big things.

Teaching and advice are important, but two other factors have an even stronger influence on young hearts and minds. The first factor is the emotional bonding between parent and child—a loving, close, trusting relationship that develops in the quantity and quality of time spent together. Much is transferred through one-on-one interaction.

Dr. Howard G. Hendricks, Dallas Theological Seminary professor, explains the power of close relationships: "You cannot motivate a person apart from intense personal relationships. You can impress someone at a distance but you can only impact him up close."[1] It's during those "up close" times with our children, when we're at home or out for a walk, at bedtime or starting the day, that we impart important spiritual messages (*see* Deuteronomy 6:6).

Second, as Jacob's and Emily's stories demonstrate, a parent's behavior or role modeling strongly influences a child. For years as an educator I observed the indelible imprint of role modeling, both at home and in the classroom. Students whose parents were enthusiastic artists and involved their children in projects tended to be excited about art. Kids whose parents wrote family newsletters or took them on cycling excursions tended to enjoy those hobbies. Children naturally assimilated their parents' interests.

Research supports this observation. One landmark study on early readers concluded that every child defined as a skilled, avid reader was influenced by parents who were frequent readers themselves and led their children by example.[2] Accordingly, almost every child I've known who was motivated to learn caught that desire from an intellectually alive parent, excited about the world of books and ideas.

Motivation for prayer is just as contagious. Kids "catch it" from parents who practice prayer—embarking on adventures with God by talking and listening to Him, being excited about praying with others, and sharing prayer with children in the spontaneous moments of living together. What if we as parents were ardent pray-ers? What if our lifestyles centered on prayer? Think how this could impact our kids!

CATCHING PRAYER IN ACTION

Kids can "catch prayer" in both the ordinary and crisis times of life. Jan Merritt was active in Moms In Touch International, leading a group of mothers who prayed for one hour weekly for their children's school. Jan received many answers to prayer, but her kids weren't learning to pray. Whenever her son Mike, age nine, or daughter Ashley, age five, encountered a problem, they asked, "Mom, would you pray about my problem at school?" "Mom, would you talk to God about my basketball tryouts?" They expected their mother to do the "prayer work" for them.

As Jan sought God about her children, she realized that she hadn't included the kids in her circle of prayer. Although she prayed with a group of women and had quiet time for reading the Bible and talking with God, the children weren't seeing their mom pray or hearing His answers. So even though her faith was increasing, the children weren't growing in prayer.

With this in mind, Jan asked God for opportunities to teach her children about prayer. The answer came quickly.

One day while her husband was out of town, Jan took her children to the San Diego Zoo. They had a wonderful day observing animals and enjoying a picnic in the sunshine. By midafternoon, hoping to avoid rush-hour traffic, Jan rounded up the kids and bundled them into the car for the drive home.

On the freeway Jan realized people were honking and pointing to her tire. She exited the freeway in front of a gated community, stepped out, and discovered a flat front tire. Jan had traveled light; all she had was a driver's license, a leftover bag of snacks, and two tired kids. She had no equipment to change the tire, no way to get into the locked gate to borrow a phone, and no husband along to help her.

Jan trudged to a beauty shop on the corner and called for help. A service station attendant said it would be at least an hour until a tow truck would arrive. Jan knew that by then the traffic would be a nightmare and the kids would be cranky. Then the thought came to her: *Call your children over to pray with you.*

She told her daughter and son about the problem, how long the wait would be, and that she had no cash or checks to pay for towing or service charges. She then asked the children to pray as they held hands in a circle by the car.

"Please send the tow truck quickly, Lord, and provide for what Mom needs to get our tire fixed," Mike prayed.

"And help Mom have a peaceful heart," Ashley added.

As they finished praying, a white tow truck pulled up.

Jan's children jumped up and down, saying, "Mom, God answers prayer quickly! Wow, look what He did!"

Within minutes the driver had changed the tire and charged Jan only $20. He was also willing to accept her credit card for payment.

The children never forgot how God answered their prayer, and the next time a need arose, they went directly to Him for help.

Shortly after that incident the Merritt family was driving back from vacation through the Mojave Desert. It was a blazing 110 degrees and nine o'clock at night. Suddenly smoke billowed from the engine and the putrid smell of burning rubber filled the air. The car died on an overpass; the fan belt had completely melted.

The family pushed the car out of the right lane and over the overpass. As Jan and her husband discussed what to do, the children jumped up and said, "Mom, let's pray! Remember what God did after our flat tire?"

So with the children leading, the family held hands. Jan and her husband didn't pray—they stood there hot and flustered while the kids bowed their heads. Full of faith, Ashley and Mike prayed expectantly for God to send help.

"We had no sooner stopped praying when out of a dirt road next to the highway came a huge van," Jan recalls. "Four large men in Air Force uniforms got out and explained that they were flying experimental helicopters and had been forced to make an emergency landing at an abandoned airstrip. They were now on the way to the next town to get pizza, and offered to give us a ride."

Although Jan felt nervous about accepting a ride from strangers, her children jumped in the military van, sure that God had answered their prayer. The pilots drove the family to town where they ate pizza together, helped purchase a fan belt, then returned to help install it on the car before waving the family on their way. Later the Merritts sent letters to the nearest Air Force base to thank them, but officials disavowed the men's existence.

To this day the children say God sent angels to rescue them on a hot desert road in the middle of nowhere!

GREAT THINGS FROM SMALL BEGINNINGS

After these "on-the-road" prayer adventures, the Merritts started a regular family prayer time. Once or twice a week, all four of them prayed together about individual and family concerns. Ashley was so excited about God's responses she wanted to record their requests and answered prayers. She created a family prayer journal and through the years, the Merritts have recorded hundreds of thanksgivings to God and built a legacy of faith together.

Now Ashley and her brother attend high school and their schedules are crazy, but the family still gathers as often as possible for that hour of prayer. Hearing their parents pray aloud for and with them through the years has left a lasting mark. Both kids are prayer leaders among their peers and serious about their relationship with God.

Jan describes the role prayer has played in her family's life: "More than anything, praying together reinforced how much we love the children and how precious they are to us. Hearing us pray for their needs and thanking God for them was very bonding. Even more than things we've given them or fun times we've spent with them, praying together made them feel loved and appreciated and cared for."

Praying *for* your children is important; it impacts them for now and eternity. But when Jan added praying *with* her children, something dynamic happened. Ashley and Mike grew as pray-ers themselves, their desire to talk and listen to God increased, and faith became more relevant to their everyday lives.

"More prayer is learned by having accessible, praying parents than by listening to preachy parents," says author V. Gilbert Beers.[3] As your children hear you pray for them and with them, they will develop a natural conversation with a heavenly Father who listens and cares.

A NATURAL, CONSISTENT HABIT

Although none of us can be perfect role models, we can make prayer a natural and consistent habit. A lifestyle of loving God and communicating with Him continually—not just talking about prayer or hearing others do it at church—makes a difference with our kids.

"Children learn from our long-term example, not from one-time actions.... Consistency is more valuable than perfection," explains Gerald Regier, former president of the Family Research Council.[4] It's the day-to-day talking and listening to God about our concerns both great and small—and bringing our kids into the circle of prayer whenever possible—that builds consistency.

David Schnorr works with an intercessory network, and since his two children were preschoolers, he's taken them to conferences, on mission trips, and to prayer congresses where he's taught and ministered to others. Caitlin and Jesse's favorite part of the conferences is the prayer ministry.

"Jesse is a normal boy and does everything other children do except he has a lot of faith and keeps me in line," says his dad. During ministry time at a church or conference, Jesse walks over to the people who've requested prayer, lays his hand on grown-ups twice his size, and intercedes for them. Adults are sometimes taken aback by how the

Holy Spirit ministers to people when this young man prays. Yet for Jesse, it's as natural to him as playing football or baseball.

"How did you raise this prayer warrior?" I asked his dad. The answer was simple.

"The way to get your kids praying is for them to see you praying, not once in a while, but regularly," David answered. "They want to imitate you and if you love the Lord and bring everything to Him in prayer, if you pray over them when they lay down to sleep, and include them when you pray for others, they just begin to do it themselves."

In her book *In My Father's House,* Corrie ten Boom revealed how the consistent model of her father's prayer life helped her learn to pray:

Every room in our house heard our prayers, but the oval table probably experienced more conversations with the Lord than other places. Praying was never an embarrassment for us, whether it was with the family together or when a stranger came in. Father prayed because he had a good Friend to talk over the problems of the day; he prayed because he had a direct connection with his Maker when he had a concern; he prayed because there was so much for which he wanted to thank God. When Father talked with the Lord it was serious, but unpretentious. He talked to Someone he knew.[5]

That was how Corrie talked to her Lord too, and through the years she affected hundreds, perhaps thousands, of people with her unique, personal style of prayer. Sometimes while talking to guests or friends she'd glance heavenward and listen to the voice of the Father. One of Corrie's friends said, "She would nod and even answer Him aloud, then very naturally [and not at all religiously] she would resume talking with us."[6]

The same heavenly Father whom her father loved became not only Corrie's Lord, but her dearest lifetime friend and confidante.

AT OUR FATHER'S KNEE
Developing our own relationship with God through prayer is key to leading children to a living faith. Francois Fénelon, a spiritual director and counselor to the court of Louis XIV in seventeenth-century France,

offered enduring advice for modern parents: "Tell [God] without hesitation everything that comes into your head, with the simplicity and familiarity of a little child sitting on its mother's knee," he advised.[7] As you grow in intimacy at your Father's knee, your love for Him will spill over to your children. You can't change their hearts and make them follow God; that's His business and their choice. But you can be a powerful role model.

Maybe you're a little frustrated, thinking "I'm not part of an intercessory organization" or "I've been like Martha, busy doing things instead of sitting at the Lord's feet and praying. Where do I start?" Start right where you are. Look for opportunities to model prayer in daily situations like car trouble, sickness, and sibling conflicts. Help your children "catch" prayer by praying with them about specific issues like friendships, school problems, and their future mates.

Look for chances to reach out to others also. Gather a few parents and pray regularly for all your kids, and in the process God will widen your heart to care about young people in your local school and community. When you visit a friend who's had surgery, let your child accompany you and ask that person how you can pray for him. If you know an elderly person in a nursing home, take your child along to visit and include prayer as part of your ministry to her. When you see someone in need, whether it's while you're driving on the freeway or watching the television news, pray for that person.

As you bring your child into your circle of prayer by interceding for and with him, God will do more than you could ever ask or think according to His power that works within you and your child (Ephesians 3:20–21).

A Prayer for the Challenge of Parenting

Heavenly Father,
Thank You that You have given me
the awesome challenge of parenting
which often drives me to my knees,
and that You don't give us a task without
having grace available for us to accomplish it.
Draw me closer to You so I can lead my children.
Grant me more desire, consistency and faithfulness in prayer.

Empower me with Your Spirit to be a praying parent,
one who not only teaches my kids faith but lives it.
Let each of my children feel an open channel with me,
their earthly father or mother,
so they will understand that they can go to You any time
and know You will lovingly listen.
In Jesus' name, Amen.

HELPING OUR KIDS PRAY

Here are some helpful suggestions for modeling prayer for your children:

- Pray conversationally. Cindy was taught only the "Now I Lay Me Down to Sleep" prayer as she was growing up. She heard an occasional rote grace said over some meals but never observed her parents praying in a conversational way. Later in her adult life, Cindy found great comfort in speaking to God as a friend. Now she wants her daughter to experience that comfort, so Cindy prays with her daughter in simple, conversational language rather than with flowery, formal words.

- Be honest with God and avoid using prayer as a guilt trip or for scolding your children. Instead of praying, "Oh, Lord, help these kids to straighten up and mind me so You won't be disappointed in them," be honest about your weakness: "Lord, forgive me for losing my temper with the children. Give me patience and Your wisdom—and fill our home with Your love and peace." Your vulnerability and willingness to receive God's help will be a greater witness to your kids than trying to be the perfect parent.

- Persevere in prayer in the prayer closet, family prayer times, and at bedtime. Let your children hear you interceding for them regularly. Let the things around you be a "cue" to pray. As you pass your children's school, ask for every student there to know Christ and for the teachers to be filled with God's wisdom. Pray for one child when you wash dishes, another when you're doing laundry. As a reminder to pray, trace each child's handprint on paper and place the drawings in your Bible or journal.

- Include your children in prayer "moments" and gatherings. Take the ordinary experiences of life—your trials and the needs of others—and turn them into "prayer moments" with your children. When there's a church prayer meeting, mission conference, or city-wide gathering for prayer, invite your children. As you do, you'll be mentoring them into a closer relationship with their heavenly Father.

Dear God,
You are wonderful and good, and you are powerful and loving! Love, Skye.

—Skye, 7

thank you good for loving us so much that you fit every piece
of the puzzle of life together exactly according to your plans.
amen!!!

—Katherine, 12

Dear Jesus,
Help me adjust to our new house and help me not to be too sad. I cannot
help crying a little bit each night, but the rest of the time I am fine. I pray in
Jesus' name, Amen.

—Camellia, 9

CHAPTER FIVE

Who Is God and Is He Listening?

*Let the little children come to me
and do not stop them,
because the kingdom of heaven
belongs to such as these.*

JESUS CHRIST

A preschool teacher taught her young students the Lord's Prayer, and each day they practiced it. One day a three-year-old volunteered to lead the class and enthusiastically prayed, "Our Father, who Artist in heaven, Halloween be Your name. Thy Kingdom come, Thy will be done, one national under God, indivisible, with livery for all. Amen!"[1]

Who is this God we address in prayer? An Artist in heaven and our Father? With these names the three year old was right on target. The "livery for all" I'm not so sure about. But since prayer is a dialogue with God, knowing Him and His attributes is important to the prayer process. John 10:4–5 says that Jesus' sheep "follow him because they know his voice." Talking to and hearing from God is about relationship, and for our children that relationship begins when they accept Christ as Savior.

When can a child come to know God through His Son, Jesus Christ? Studies show that most children who receive Christ do so between the ages of four and fourteen,[2] so the early years are a golden opportunity for faith to root and grow. "Children are natural seekers," says Karyn Henley, educator and author of *Child-Sensitive Teaching*. "They just need us to point the way."[3]

When Corrie ten Boom was five years old, she learned to read and love stories—especially stories about Jesus. Describing her relationship with Christ, she recalls, "He was a member of the ten Boom family—it was just as easy to talk to Him as it was to carry on a conversation with my mother and father, my aunts, or my brother and sisters. He was there."

Corrie's mother pointed her to Jesus in a gentle, child-sensitive way. One day Mrs. ten Boom was watching little Corrie, who was playing house and pretending to call on a neighbor. Corrie knocked on the make-believe door and waited, but no one answered.

Corrie's mother patiently watched her daughter play. "Corrie, I know Someone who is standing at your door and knocking right now," said Mrs. ten Boom.

Corrie describes the moment: "Was she playing a game with me? I know now that there was a preparation within my childish heart for that moment. The Holy Spirit makes us ready for acceptance of Jesus Christ, of turning our life over to Him."

Her mother continued, "Jesus said that He is standing at the door, and if you invite Him in He will come into your heart. Would you like to invite Jesus in?"

"Yes, Mama, I want Jesus in my heart," young Corrie answered.

Corrie's mother took her daughter's hand and they prayed together. "It was so simple," Corrie reflects, "and yet Jesus Christ says that we all must come as children, no matter what our age, social standing, or intellectual background."[4]

Was she too young for that decision? Did Corrie know what she was doing? From that point on, Jesus became more of a reality to her and she began interceding for others, especially the poor people of the Smedestraat, a rough area near their street where people got drunk and were arrested for crimes. Corrie became so burdened for these people, she wept and prayed for them while passing the street, asking God to save them.

Years later Corrie went camping with eighteen girls who had all lived in the city and become Christians. While visiting with them, Corrie discovered that the girls or their parents had lived in the Smedestraat. God had used the prayers of a small child to reach them!

"Never doubt whether God hears our prayers, even the unusual ones," she says. And never doubt that He listens and responds to the prayers of a child![5] No matter their size or age, "when a believing person prays, great things happen" (James 5:16b, NCV).

GOD'S YOUNG WARRIORS

When mothers brought their children to Jesus so He could bless and touch them, the disciples tried to shoo them away, rebuking the moms for their intrusion. When Jesus saw this, He was indignant and upset, not with the mothers and children, but with His disciples. He said, "Let the little children come to Me, and do not hinder them, because the kingdom of God belongs to such as these" (Mark 10:13–16). Because Jesus accepts our children as He did those young ones on the hillside centuries ago, they can readily respond to His love in a variety of settings. Kids can accept Christ as Savior through many kinds of creative means, and they don't necessarily have to be at church to do it.

For example, Zack, a four year old, accepted Christ at home by learning about the "armor" described in Ephesians 6. His mom, Connie, had been studying spiritual warfare in a Bible study, so she thought it would make a good topic for home schooling. Connie helped her two children cut up huge boxes, fit and glue pieces together, and paint them bright colors. She identified pieces as the "Sword of the Spirit," "Shield of Faith," and "Helmet of Salvation," and explained what they represented.

"We need to know the Bible to combat the enemy's darts," the mother began. "The Helmet of Salvation means accepting Jesus as your Savior. Having the assurance that you belong to Him protects your mind." The helmets were the children's favorite part of the "armor suits." Decorations squirted out the top of Zack's head gear like the plume on a Roman soldier's helmet, and paper flowers graced three-year-old Kathryn's helmet.

Zachary embraced the warrior idea and loved wearing his armor, even after he and his sister began studying another topic. One night at bedtime prayers, he told his mom he wanted to be a real warrior with Jesus as his commander. He wanted to invite the Lord into his heart. Through this simple activity and teaching, Zack heard Christ knocking and opened the door to his Savior. He soon led his younger sister to the Lord and began praying for friends and family.

Zachary's desire to introduce his sister and others to Christ typifies young children's response to salvation. Kids want to share the good news in their lives with the people they love. They want others to love Jesus, and this desire easily leads to simple prayers and evangelism.

One night when the Browns conducted bedtime prayers with their two children, TJ and Hannah, four-year-old TJ leaned over to his two-and-a-half-year-old sister and said, "You know, Hannah, I've been thinking that everyone in this family is going to heaven—everyone except you. I want you to go to heaven and not hell, and you need to ask Jesus into your heart."

This sensitive toddler replied, "I want to go to heaven too. I want Daddy to pray with me now."

Hannah's dad talked to her on several occasions following that night about why Jesus came to earth, what it means to have an unclean, sinful heart, and how to accept Jesus and grow in a relationship with Him. In the course of their conversations, Hannah seemed to understand and acknowledge her need for a clean heart. On her own initiative, she started confessing sins—her mean thoughts about her brother when he didn't share, how she'd taken a cookie when her parents weren't looking, and others. After much dialogue Hannah's parents felt she understood salvation and prayed with her to receive Christ.

Soon Hannah started telling people about Jesus who "lives in her heart," and how He can live in them too. Some may question whether such a young child could truly understand conversion, but Hannah has stuck with her commitment. Now eight years old, she still has a heart for God and is growing in her relationship with Him. Recently Hannah was baptized and said she wants to serve the Lord as a missionary.

GUIDING A CHILD TO GOD

A few days after six-year-old Bryant decided to follow Christ, he was outside, lying in his huge wagon, gazing up at the sky. Then suddenly he walked into the house, tears streaming down his cheeks. Bryant's dad followed him into his room and asked, "What's wrong, Son?"

"Daddy, sometimes does it just make you want to cry when you think about Jesus dying on the cross to pay for our sins?" Little Bryant was overcome by the love of God for sinful people, including himself.

Bryant's mom and dad had prayed since their son's birth that he would want a personal relationship with Christ. They knew their prayers had been answered.

There are distinct stages in children's spiritual growth, and understanding these can help you in leading them to Christ. As a children's pastor at First Baptist Church of Orlando, Florida, Art Murphy has counseled thousands of kids and has baptized more than 1000 of them. He encourages parents not to push their children toward commitment or baptism, but not to turn them away, either. Instead, Art advises holding out your hand and leading them as they move through faith development. As Murphy describes in his video, "First Steps: Leading Your Child to Christ," there are four stages of spiritual development:[6]

1. The Discovery Stage

From birth to age seven, children are constantly discovering new information and soaking up everything in their environment—things they see and experience, parents' and siblings' behavior, the Bible stories being read to them.

Scripture reveals that Timothy's mother and grandmother taught him during his early years. "From infancy you have known the holy Scriptures," wrote Paul to young Timothy, who played an important role in early church history. Little by little character forms and faith emerges in the Discovery Stage.

Tender and innocent little ones may not understand all the spiritual words they hear at home or in Sunday school, but they record this information in their sharp memories and later might repeat them verbatim. Many young children ask questions. Others may not be able to verbalize their ideas. All are still thinking and observing.

2. The Discerning Stage

This second stage begins in the early elementary years, ages four to eight, where kids increasingly ask pointed questions. "What happens when Grandpa dies?" "Where is heaven?" "How do I get to go to heaven?" They've heard spiritual concepts and Bible stories and start personalizing things by wondering, "How does this apply to me?" Notice the overlap with the Discovery Stage. Because children are unique, some may stay in the Discovery Stage until age seven, while other five year olds have already reached the Discerning Stage.

Murphy calls this the "kick in the womb" stage. The kicks (or questions) aren't labor pains, but they indicate that the child is starting the journey and is interested in knowing more about God. Sometimes a parent thinks the questions indicate the child's readiness for commitment, so he rushes ahead and asks the pastor, "Can you baptize him this Sunday?" Murphy tells the eager parent, "Life's coming, but it may not be delivery time yet."

At this stage it's important for parents and other adults to help kids learn about Jesus and model vibrant faith, but to also discern God's timing. "We're the pediatricians but God is the obstetrician. He has their spiritual birth planned just as He did their physical birth," says Murphy.

During this stage children still might only be repeating what they've heard from adults or older kids and they may not yet understand spiritual terminology. A nervous seven-year-old girl, visiting church for the first time, walked to the altar and said, "I want to ask Jesus into my stomach." A Jewish girl who had attended church with a neighbor family approached the altar and told the pastor, "I want to ask Jesus into my heart. But can I ask Moses into my heart too? 'Cause I know him much better."

While children can have a genuine salvation experience at this stage, we can't assume that each one understands the invitation at the end of a service and is ready to commit to Christ. We need dialogue, prayer, and discernment to gauge a child's spiritual awareness.

3. The Deciding Stage

The Deciding Stage draws a line between children's curiosity and conviction. For example, a ten-year-old girl remembers, "When I was five years old I tried to become a Christian but my pastor said I was too young. I was real upset but don't remember much about it. My parents said, 'Be patient. Let's learn about God together. He has a just-right time for you.'"

What seemed like "a good thing to do" at age five became a sincere commitment at age nine. She understood that salvation meant surrender to God, and one day on the way home from church she prayed, asking Christ into her heart. The next week the girl's parents walked with her to the altar. She attended a new members' class, talked to the pastor, and was baptized. She had found God's "just right time" for salvation.

4. The Discipleship Stage

"It may take about fifteen minutes to get a child to Christ, but it takes about five years to make him a disciple," says Murphy. While many children will make a commitment to Christ between ages seven to thirteen, these are crucial years for grounding them in their faith, teaching them to pray, and helping them know God better. It's vital to help them walk out their decision to follow Christ, develop healthy spiritual habits, and to be accountable, especially before they become teenagers.

As a child passes through these stages, parents and teachers can provide opportunities that enhance the faith development process. Asking questions and praying with your child will help you know where he stands spiritually. Enjoy talking with your child about everyday things, not just spiritual concepts. Avoid lecturing but instead listen, talk, pray, and ask questions.

Even a simple question like, "Could you draw me a picture of how you're feeling about God and where you are with Him?" offers valuable insight. When I asked our three children this question in a family devotional time, Alison, age ten, drew a big heart and a little girl on the inside of it (who looked just like her). "That's me, right inside God's heart because He loves me," she explained. Chris, thirteen, drew a detailed picture of a brick window ledge and a boy just barely hanging on to the windowsill. "That's how I feel right now with all the changes of moving here (to Maine from Oklahoma) and a new school. I'm hanging on to God." However, our fifteen-year-old son held up a blank piece of paper and asked to be excused. From that simple exercise and conversation, my husband and I discerned each child's spiritual condition.

In her book, *Teaching Your Child to Talk to God,* Roberta Hromas emphasizes the importance of devotional times with our kids. Throughout her children's growing up years she prayed regularly with them. "I wouldn't let more than three days go by without hearing them pray," she writes. "I'd let them get by with silent prayers or 'I don't want to pray' responses for no longer than three days, and then I cancelled all my plans, and theirs. We would spend a delightful time together talking about the wonderful ways of Jesus. By evening time the kids' personal relationship with the Lord was renewed and they'd be eager to pray aloud." Hromas believes kids prayers are a spiritual barometer of their relationship with the Lord.[7]

Church activities also help your children grow closer to God. When they can fellowship, pray, and learn about God with other kids, Christian friendships develop. They belong to a community of believers—something bigger than themselves—and learn to care for others outside the family.

When we expose a child to spiritual growth opportunities, we may not see immediate results, but with time, prayer, and patience, we can reap the joy of our work. Our children may even begin praying for and ministering to us!

KIDS MINISTERING TO ADULTS

It's amazing how a connection to the true Source of life fires up a prayer life, whether you're thirteen or forty-three. Although Jonathan and his parents had prayer time during the family's regular Bible study, he felt self-conscious and inadequate about praying aloud. His parents had prayed out loud for and with him his whole life, and he had accepted Christ as his Savior. But Jonathan didn't think he could pray "good prayers" like his parents, so sometimes he wouldn't even try. When he did pray, it was as short as possible: "Thank You, God, for this day."

When Jonathan was twelve years old, he recommitted his life to Christ at a youth gathering and realized he needed to develop his own relationship with God instead of riding on his parents' spiritual coattails. He continued to learn God's Word and pray with his parents, but what really reinforced his growth was the youth group at church where kids prayed for each other. As Jonathan joined in, God answered quickly and the boy grew more confident in his prayers. A "Teen Mania" conference bolstered his faith even more, and since then he has enjoyed regular personal devotions with his heavenly Father. Gradually Jonathan's self-consciousness is growing into a God-consciousness.

Recently Jonathan's mom, Jan, was driving on the busy Interstate with her son beside her. Jan became upset that three other drivers were urgently trying to pass her car, tailgating her and changing lanes quickly without signaling. She reacted to the other drivers' poor driving with anger and frustration. To console his mother, Jonathan placed his hand lightly on her arm and prayed aloud for God to give her peace.

Jan immediately felt better, as well as repentant! The sense of urgency that seemed to rule the highway didn't trouble her anymore. They drove to their friends' house safely and peacefully, and Jan enjoyed the day much more than if she'd arrived feeling angry and impatient. Her young son had ministered to his mother that day.

UNDERSTANDING WHO GOD IS

The more children understand who God is, the more confidently they can pray. When we pray for His peace, we're not asking Him for something outside His capabilities, because God is peace and Jesus is the Prince of Peace. When we ask Him to provide for a need, we do it with confidence because He is the Lord, our Provider.

Consequently, learning God's attributes and names can be an exciting boost to your child's prayer life. In fact, the British preacher Charles Spurgeon encouraged "pleading God's attributes" as David did in Psalm 51:1: "Have mercy on me, O God, according to your unfailing love; according to your great compassion blot out my transgressions." Spurgeon said, "Faith will plead all the attributes of God—You are good, reveal Your bounty to Your servant; You are immutable—You have done this for others of your servants; do it for me."[8]

The Bible is a great resource for this endeavor. The Psalms declare, "the LORD is gracious and compassionate...holy and awesome is his name" (Psalm 111:4, 9). Children can tell God they love Him by describing who He is:

- *He is Jehovah-nissi,* The Lord My Banner, and His banner over us is love (Exodus 17:15; Song of Songs 2:4).
- *He is Jehovah-jireh,* The Lord Will Provide, and He knows our needs and provides for them (Genesis 22:14).
- *He is Jehovah-shalom,* The Lord Is Peace, who gives us inner peace (Judges 6:24).

- *He is Jehovah-raah,* The Lord My Shepherd, who promises to lead and guide us, to speak to us and show us what direction to go (Psalm 23:1).
- *He is Jehovah-rapha,* the Lord Who Heals (Psalm 103:3; 147:3).
- *He is Jehovah-tsidkenu,* The Lord Our Righteousness (Jeremiah 23:6). Because of Jesus, God forgives our sins.
- *He is Jehovah-shammah,* The Lord Is There, so that we can confidently say, "The Lord is my Helper! I will not fear or dread or be terrified" (Hebrews 13:6, AMP).

Wherever our children go, God is with them. This is great news, no matter their age. Psalm 9:10 says, "Those who know your name will put their trust in you, for you, Lord, have never forsaken those who seek you." Helping your children know His names and attributes will grow their trust and faith—and greatly enrich their prayer life.

Another creative way to help children know God better is by playing "Alphabet Praise."

Forty energetic children from kindergarten to fourth grade wiggled in the folding chairs for children's church one autumn Sunday. "Let's praise God today from A to Z," I suggested. "He's so great and mighty we could describe Him all day, but we just have an hour. So let's start with 'A.' Raise your hand if you know something about God that starts with an 'A!'"

The wheels turned in their heads and soon the hands shot up.

"Awesome! God's awesome!" said one little boy.

"Able! He's able to do anything!" said another.

"Authority," said a serious-looking girl wearing glasses. "He's got all the authority."

I wrote the words on a white board as fast as the kids called the words out. We finished with "A," covered "B," then started on "C."

"Creator!"

"He's compassionate!"

"He comforts us!"

"Cind!" two boys said in unison.

"Cind?" I explained that this was really a "K" word, but agreed that God is really kind.

The kids surprised me with how much they knew about God. He's caring, He's our Counselor. He's our deliverer. God is our Father, our friend, a fortress. He's the King of kings and yes, He's kind! He's life, light, love, and loyal to His people. Sovereign, Savior, supreme, and our shield. It took two Sundays to complete the whole alphabet, and all the while we were praising God aloud for His wonderful attributes.

"What comes into our minds when we think about God is the most important thing about us," wrote A. W. Tozer. He believed having a right concept of God was basic to living the Christian life. And to usher spiritual power into our prayers, "we must begin to think of God more nearly as He is" as we step into His presence.[9]

A Prayer for Knowing God

Lord, I want my children to know You
and put their trust in You.
I ask You to reveal Yourself to my kids
and to help me discern what You are doing
in each stage of their journey.
Give me patience with their questions and wisdom to answer them,
along with the grace and faith to always point them
to You and Your Word.
Thank You for putting eternity in their hearts,
for creating within them a space that only You can fill!
In Jesus' name, Amen.

HELPING KIDS PRAY

You can help your child grow in knowledge and understanding of God by making a notebook about His character. Each page can feature a different letter of the alphabet and include Scripture verses about who God is. Then, choose one attribute to focus on each week. Use a concordance to look up verses on a specific attribute, and praise God together for that part of His nature.

Encourage your child to write in his own words the truths he's discovering about God's character or his "favorite things" about God. Soon God's attributes will come alive in your child's life.[10] Here are some attributes and qualities to help your child get started.

A: Able, Available, Advocate

B: Beloved, Beauty, Bridegroom

C: Creator, Compassionate, Commander, Comforter, Counselor

D: Deliverer, Defender

E: Eternal, Exalted, Everlasting

F: Faithful, Forgiving, Friend

G: Gentle, Grace, Giver, Guide

H: High Priest, Holy, Husband

I: Indwelling, Inviting

J: Just

K: Keeper, King, Kind

L: Light, Life, Love

M: Maker, Merciful, Majestic

N: Nourishment

O: Owner, Omnipotent, Omniscient

P: Promise Keeper, Protector, Provider, Powerful

Q: Quiet

R: Refuge, Reward

S: Shepherd, Sovereign, Strength, Sufficiency

T: Teacher, Truth

U: Unchangeable

V: Victor, Virtuous

W: Wonderful Counselor, Worthy

X: X-tra good! X-ellent!

Y: the same Yesterday, today, and forever

Z: Zealous

CHAPTER SIX

Stepping into God's Presence

A prayer prayed from the heart of the child
to the Father is never in vain.

ELISABETH ELLIOT

Children and parents bustled about the Israeli market created for the "Bible Times" Vacation Bible School at Our Lord's Community Church in Oklahoma City. Dressed in togas and robes, they roamed from the jewelry maker's to the carpentry shop, watching craftsmen work and stopping to try leather making, weaving, or pottery. Israeli music rang out from the speakers and a food booth offered snacks to the curious crowd.

When several children discovered the prayer booth, they walked between two facing benches draped with colorful paisley fabric. The benches represented the Outer Court of the Tabernacle, a place where the Old Testament Israelites met with God. As the children moved through each part of the Tabernacle, they learned about entering into God's presence. They also had a chance to experience the Lord's presence for themselves.

In the Outer Court, Sandy, their "tour guide," led the children in a song of praise and read verses about entering God's courts with praise. She then accompanied them to an imaginative version of the Brazen Altars, where spotless lambs were sacrificed as atonement for people's sins. Sandy explained the altar's purpose and the children, taking their brief pilgrimage to heart, surrendered themselves to God and confessed their sins.

"The Holy Spirit will remind you about what things in your life you need to confess and be cleansed of so you can receive God's forgiveness," Sandy reminded them as they passed a homemade replica of the laver, a bowl of water used by the priests to wash their hands. She then read Scriptures about forgiveness as the children washed their hands in the laver.

"Before Christ came to the earth the Tabernacle was a physical meeting place where the priests ministered to God," Sandy continued. "But because of Christ, we are God's dwelling place and we are priests who can enter His presence and minister to Him." With this explanation, she opened the door to the Holy Place, the dimly lit prayer room displaying bread (representing the loaves of shewbread the priests ate) and a Jewish menora. In this room they read aloud verses about Jesus: "I am the bread of life. He who comes to me will never go hungry, and he who believes in me will never be thirsty" (John 6:35).

When the children lit the menora (representing the golden lampstand in the temple, also symbolic of the Holy Spirit), they heard Jesus' words again: "I am the light of the world" (John 8:12). They asked Jesus to bring His light into their world, and for Him to be their bread; in other words, the most important person in their life.

Next they entered the Holy of Holies, the most sacred place, where God spoke to the high priest only once a year. Sandy explained, "It's wonderful that God doesn't speak to us only one time a year like in the Old Testament, but many times." She encouraged the children to close their eyes and imagine the Holy of Holies, where the ark of the covenant stood. "Pure gold covered the wooden box that contained the rod of Aaron, the manna, and the Ten Commandments," she taught them. And they pictured the mercy seat, adorned with golden cherubim on top of the ark, and learned that it represents God's grace toward us through Christ's sacrifice.

At this point Sandy invited the kids to draw near to God, asking Him to show them His glory. "He invites you to come to His throne of grace with full assurance, because you can talk to God about the things on your heart and pray for people you're concerned about," she said. Peace and quiet filled the room. Several children knelt and tarried, while others prayed more quickly and left.

This Tabernacle journey created a pattern for the children to help them step away from the noise and hustle of the market into the quiet awe of God's presence. In a similar way, this is the purpose of a prayer model: It moves us from the noise and busyness of our world into a place where we can talk and listen to God. A prayer model can lead children through the key elements of prayer so they can communicate with Him, but at the same time, it isn't a rigid formula that squelches spontaneity. Rather, a model aids the understanding of prayer's wondrous components.

HOW JESUS TAUGHT US TO PRAY

When the disciples implored, "Lord, teach us how to pray" (Luke 11:1, Phillips), Jesus responded by providing a prayer model for His followers, found in Matthew 6:9–13 and Luke 11:1–4. We can use the same Lord's Prayer to help our children learn to pray.

Honor God's Name

Before we plunge into our requests, Jesus suggested that we first pray "Hallowed be your name" (Matthew 6:9) which means "May Your name be honored." Essentially, He was saying, "Before you rush in to ask God for what you need, express your praise for who He is. Remember that God is your heavenly Father, He loves you, and wants you to come to Him." You can prompt children to pause and praise God's name by saying, "Father God, I praise You that You are holy, awesome, and full of lovingkindness. Thank You that You hear me when I pray."

Embrace God's Will

Jesus said to pray, "Your kingdom come, your will be done on earth as it is in heaven" (Matthew 6:10). When kids pray these words, they're learning to yield to God's will and plan. You can model this attitude to children by praying, "Lord, whatever happens today, may all You have planned come to pass. I surrender and respond to Your will because You know the future. You know what is best!" This is submission— trusting God and laying down our lives. It may sound difficult, but actually it's exciting—because we're asking for God's divine intervention on our behalf.

Ask for What We Need

When we pray "Give us today our daily bread" (Matthew 6:11), we're requesting all that we need physically, spiritually, and emotionally to do what He has called us to accomplish. Kids can depend on God for all their needs and tell Him what's on their hearts. This open communication encourages them. In Matthew 6:8 Jesus said, "Your Father knows what you need before you ask him," but He requires that we ask, seek, and knock to get answers. (See the verses about persistent prayer in Luke 11:5–10.)

Forgive and Be Forgiven

"Forgive us our debts, as we also have forgiven our debtors" (Matthew 6:12). This is the part of prayer when we confess our sins and receive forgiveness for how we have hurt others, and forgive those who have sinned against us. A few verses later Jesus reiterates how important it is to forgive others: "For if you forgive men when they sin against you, your heavenly Father will also forgive you. But if you do not forgive men their sins, your Father will not forgive your sins" (Matthew 6:14–15). This is great motivation for not holding on to resentment or bitterness, and the sooner children embrace this principle the more their souls will flourish as they grow older.

Ask Protection from Evil

In this part of prayer we step under God's umbrella, asking for guidance and protection from evil. We also need His deliverance to lead us out of temptation that deceives and draws us away from His path. By praying "And lead us not into temptation, but deliver us from the evil one" (Matthew 6:13), we acknowledge our dependence on God's saving power and invoke His protection. And how we need it!

Say "Amen!"

Children love saying "Amen" but often don't know what it means. Every night when my friend Pam said bedtime prayers with her two-year-old son, Ben, he would end his prayer with "A'mee" instead of "Amen." Pam couldn't figure out why he used that benediction, until she compared notes with his best friend Amy's mom. She laughed, explaining that her daughter ended prayers with, "A'Ben!" You might explain to slightly older children that "Amen" means "So be it!"

As you pray the Lord's Prayer with your young "disciples," pause at any point to let them share their thoughts with God. Give them the freedom to express each part of the prayer model with their unique style. "God receives us just as we are and accepts our prayers just as they are," claims author Richard Foster. "In the same way that a small child cannot draw a bad picture, so a child of God cannot offer a bad prayer."[1] With this kind of freedom in prayer, you'll observe children stepping toward God's throne to love and enjoy Him.

THE ACTS MODEL

When teaching kids to pray, I've also found the ACTS model to be helpful. It consists of a simple four-part process of Adoration, Confession, Thanksgiving, and Supplication, similar to the "Four Steps of Prayer" used by Moms In Touch International and other prayer groups.

Adoration

Adoration means to "love God with all the power within us."[2] Not just acknowledging Him as the ultimate Need Meeter, but expressing our love and devotion through praise, Scripture, vocal and instrumental music, and other celebrations of God's majesty. Adoration, or worship, should begin almost any model of prayer because we first want God to know how much we love Him.

Worship ushers us into deeper prayer. Evangelist R. A. Torrey emphasized, "We are saved not just to serve God but to worship.... Prayer will find its freest access to the Throne of Grace and will be accompanied by the fullest assurance and joy when it is preceded by a time of true worship of God."[3]

Kids can worship God privately or together in groups. Group settings are often more conducive, because group worship cultivates camaraderie and builds momentum. (Some kids feel less inhibited if they can get "lost" in a group.) Children can worship by saying one sentence aloud to tell God what they love about Him or what they're grateful for; by playing rhythm instruments and singing praise with a cassette tape while marching in a circle; by kneeling or standing reverently to show honor to God as they pray; or by reading aloud from the Psalms in a chorus fashion. (Try Psalm 92, 98, 100, 101, 115, 117, or 144–150.)

If you pray the Psalms with kids, don't be caught up in the form. Eugene Peterson, author of The Message paraphrase of the Bible, reassures us that "God hears anything we whisper or shout, say or sing. Right words and correct forms are not prerequisite to a heavenly audience...all the same, the Psalms are necessary...they are God's gift to train us in prayer."[4] Jesus Himself prayed the Psalms, so kids are in good company when they speak these poems and songs back to God.

Confession

No matter our age, confession is a key component in prayer. We can ask our child or group of children, "What are some wrong things we do that grieve God or make Him sad—sins we commit that might need to be confessed?" Then provide examples: being mean to a sister, tattling on her, talking back to Mom, acting jealous, or staying angry at a friend. We can lead them to silently pick one thing that comes to mind that could be honestly confessed before God.

God longs to hear from His children, but the lines of communication clog up with unconfessed sin—anger, unforgiveness, wrong thoughts and actions, or a variety of spiritual offenses. Confession reopens the communication lines so we can hear God as we pray. David declared in Psalm 66:18, "If I had cherished [harbored or held] sin in my heart, the Lord would not have listened."

After silent confession time, children can be reassured from 1 John 1:9: "If we confess our sins, he is faithful and just and will forgive us our sins and purify us from all unrighteousness." That's great reason for...

Thanksgiving

Many places in Scripture God reminds us to be thankful, but we're especially to be grateful when we pray. For example, in Philippians 4:6–9 Paul admonished Christians to have no anxiety about anything, but to pray about everything. With thanksgiving, Paul writes, we are to present our requests to God. An attitude of gratitude is God's will for us (1 Thessalonians 5:18); He wants us to always be thankful, and it is a door through which we enter His presence (Psalm 100:4).

An essential part of prayer is simply saying, "Thank You, God!" If you're leading a group of children, ask them to think of the blessings God has given them, like a nice teacher, a new pet, Mommy and Daddy, recovery from illness, or winning a baseball game. Prompt them to be thankful to God for the everyday things they appreciate.

Jan Merritt, in her *Prayer Kids* notebook, offers verses that express thanksgiving for different blessings and encourages children to write or say a "Thank You, God" prayer for each of them. She includes these suggestions:

- *Your Word, the Bible.* "Your word is a lamp to my feet and a light for my path" (Psalm 119:105). "Thank You for Your Word, the Bible, that helps me each day to live for You. When I don't know what to do, I can find an answer in Your Word."
- *Your creation, the world.* "God saw all that he had made, and it was very good" (Genesis 1:31). "Thank You, Lord, for creating such a beautiful world, for the trees, the birds, all of the animals and plants, and for creating all the people. You've given us a wonderful place to live!"
- *Your child, me.* "I praise You because I am fearfully and wonderfully made" (Psalm 139:14). "Thank You for making me just as I am. I know I am a wonderful creation because You tell me so. You know me so well. You even know every hair on my head."

Supplication

The root word of "supplication" is "supply." Making supplication is asking God to supply our needs, but also bringing Him the hurts, pains, and needs of others. When kids "make supplication" they can ask God to help Grandma who is in the hospital. They can also pray for their own needs, for a friend, for help in learning a school task, for the desire to obey, or for courage and strength in a difficult time.

When kids plug into supplication for themselves and others, unusual things happen. Katherine Saunders, a twelve year old from Hornsby, New South Wales, was asked to pray that a woman's house would sell. Katherine didn't know the woman, but when she prayed and asked God to send His Holy Spirit to help, the situation changed quickly. Katherine explains:

I started praying like never before and the words came forth like a gurgling river. I asked God to touch her and to do His will. About five weeks later, I received the news that her house had been on the real estate market for five years, and only one week after I prayed for her, it was sold! God catered to my prayers down to every detail. The lady had wanted the new owners to not just like the house, but to truly enjoy it. That's exactly what the new owners said. This was the first time I had experienced a big answer to my prayers.

Between steps in the prayer process, encourage children to wait on God to hear what He wants them to pray, and to receive guidance from His Spirit. After the prayer time the children can write down their prayer requests, date them, and record the answer later. Then they can thank God for His goodness and, as they express their gratitude, move from wonder to worship.

A Prayer for God's Presence

Thank You, Lord, for the prayer models
You've provided in Your Word—
patterns that show us how to step from our busy world
and crowded thoughts into Your presence.
Give me grace to use these models and lead children in prayer,
not with rigidity, but with freedom and openness of heart,
always keeping my eyes fixed on Jesus,
the Author and Finisher of our faith.
In His Name, Amen.

HELPING KIDS PRAY

Prayer models for children can be simple and fun. Try these to keep them interested in talking to God.

- The J-O-Y way of praying. A simple but helpful model for young children follows the J-O-Y pattern, which stands for Jesus—Others—Yourself.
  - J – Jesus. Tell Jesus you love Him and focus on how good, loving and kind He is, His blessings, His character—that Christ is the Prince of Peace, our Savior, and Friend. Say "Thank you!" to Jesus for His love, and love Him with praise.

O – *Others.* Is there someone who needs God's help? Someone you are concerned about or who doesn't know Jesus? A missionary family in another country? Pray for them.

Y – *Yourself.* Is there something you need to tell God you're sorry for? Or specific needs or concerns?

- The "Prayer Sandwich." Sometimes we need a concrete or hands-on activity to communicate to children the parts of the prayer process. Here's a delightful and edible method that Jill Harris, Children's Mission education specialist in Atlanta, has used with hundreds of children.[5]

   Buy a large unsliced loaf such as French bread. Cut the loaf in half and lay the bottom down flat. As you add each ingredient to the sandwich, pray according to the following model:

Bottom piece of bread: "Dear God…"
Lettuce: Praise
Tomatoes: Thanksgiving
Pickles: Confession
Cold Cuts: Petitions
Cheese: Intercession
Mayo: Protection
Top piece: "In Jesus' name, Amen."

   You can reduce the number of ingredients in the "Prayer Sandwich" according to the age of the children, then add more as they grow in their ability to focus and wait before they eat. You can also adapt the "Prayer Sandwich" to any prayer models of your choice. When you're finished praying, slice up the sandwiches and enjoy!

- "Call and Response" Prayers. With this activity, a leader prays aloud a phrase (such as a paraphrase of each line of the Lord's Prayer) and then the children pray it aloud to God. This type of prayer allows children and teenagers to experience corporate prayer and hear their own voices aloud in front of others. As they grow accustomed to hearing themselves pray, they become more confident praying with a group.[6]

   Most of all, encourage children to pray from their hearts. Assure them that God loves them and wants to hear their voices and answer their prayers.

Dear God,
Help the children in other countries to know Jesus and please show them you love them. Amen.

—Trey, 6

lord,
you know my heart. you know the burden i have for the lost and hurting. i pray that you will use me in an awesome and wonderful way. even though i am young and still learning more each day about you. i trust in you to guide me in all my steps. i pray that you will open the lost people's eyes so they can see your love through me. continue to mold me into your image. i love you with all that i am and thank you for your unconditional love!

—Elisha, 16

Dear God,
I'm thankful for faith in Christ and for my sister and the joy that you give me in my heart. And I want you to know that I love you very much.

—Abigail, 7

CHAPTER SEVEN

From Wonder to Worship

The greatest poem ever known
Is one all poets have outgrown:
The poetry, innate, untold,
Of being only four years old.

CHRISTOPHER MORLEY

Thirty years ago as the Herndons were building their new home overlooking a lake, Dad would scoop Mom and the kids into the car after work and take them to see what the construction workers had accomplished that day.

One spring night the sun was setting and Mark, two years old, looked up at the red, purple, and gold sunset. Filled with awe and wonder, he knelt in the weeds and said, "Thank You, Jesus! Oh, Mama, the sunset's so bootiful!" As the toddler worshiped God for the sky's beauty, his mom knelt beside him and joined in.

Mark's spontaneous worship recalls the verse in which Jesus said, "From the mouths of children and babies I'll furnish a place of praise" (Matthew 21:16, *The Message*). When Jesus entered Jerusalem for the last time, young people stood among those praising Him, shouting "Hosanna to the Son of David!" (Matthew 21:9). As He drove out the moneychangers and healed the blind and the lame, children shouted His praises (Matthew 21:15). The religious grown-ups, chief priests, and scribes, however, were indignant. Consequently, Jesus rebuked them, explaining that He had provided praise to Himself through the children (Matthew 21:16).

Centuries earlier David had expressed in the Psalms, "Many, O Lord my God, are the wonders you have done" (Psalm 40:5) and "The heavens declare the glory of God; and the skies proclaim the work of his hands" (Psalm 19:1). But even with the Creator passing among them, adults who saw Jesus missed their "cue" to marvel and worship. Instead, it was the children and youth who spilled forth the praise.

TRAILING CLOUDS OF GLORY

At the Herndon's construction site, a toddler's childlike wonder at the sky led to brief moments of worship. Once we experience wonder and begin to worship, we're ushered into God's presence and meaningful prayer.

"The first mood of prayer—the ground from which all the rest must grow—is certainly worship, awe, adoration; delight in that holy reality for its own sake," writes Evelyn Underhill in *The Love of God*.[1] Often kids experience life's wonder and God's "awesomeness" better than adults do. They can see the extraordinary in the ordinary.

Where does a child's holy sense of wonder come from? In his poem "Ode on Intimations of Immortality," the British poet William Wordsworth provides an insightful explanation:

> Our birth is but a sleep and a forgetting
> The Soul that rises with us, our life's Star,
> hath had elsewhere its setting,
> And cometh from afar:
> Not in entire forgetfulness,
> And not in utter nakedness,
> But trailing clouds of glory do we come
> From God, who is our home:
> Heaven lies about us in our infancy![2]

Wordsworth understood something about the special vision and wonder that little ones, who aren't long from their heavenly home, possess. For many of us, that wonder fades as we grow up. We over-schedule our day-planners, think we've seen and done everything and that nothing will surprise us. But children, "trailing clouds of glory," enjoy a special awe that sometimes helps them see what adults don't notice or perhaps cannot see.

One day when my friend Sheila drove her three-year-old son Morgan to preschool, he gazed out the window from the confines of his car seat.

"Mommy, what is the white part in the sky?" Morgan asked.

"Those are clouds," Sheila answered.

"And what's *that?*" he inquired, pointing to something in the sky.

"What?" she replied offhandedly. She couldn't see anything but a cloud formation in the blue sky.

"Oh, Mom, that's heaven! Look! There's Jesus! There's everybody!" Morgan exclaimed.

Sheila strained her neck, trying hard to identify what her son saw without wrecking the car.

"Oh, there's Jesus, healing Grandpa Phil! He's touching him and Grandpa's smiling!"

Sheila couldn't see Morgan's vision of heaven, but she and her husband Lance were powerfully encouraged by it. Eight years earlier, five years before Morgan was born, his grandfather Phil died after a massive heart attack at age fifty. Phil hadn't talked about his faith and Lance wasn't certain about his dad's relationship with Christ. He only knew there were broken places in his dad's life that had desperately needed God's healing. Left with a nagging worry about whether or not his dad had entered heaven, Lance asked God to give him assurance about Phil's home in the afterlife. When Morgan told his dad what he had seen—his grandpa with Jesus—for the first time Lance felt assured and peaceful about his dad's destination.

Maybe children's wonder relates to the fact that they recognize their dependency, whereas adults often feel self-sufficient and in control. "Wonder, like all childlike qualities, grows out of humility. Wonder comes only to the ones who see how big God is and how little we are," says Alan D. Wright in *A Chance at Childhood Again.*[3] Children humbly accept their "smallness" compared to God's "bigness."

Andrew, a preschooler I know, is fascinated by the night sky. "I can't touch the moon and stars, but God can!" he told his mom Chantel while gazing up into the heavens one evening.

On an outing to the lake to feed the ducks, Chantel had shared with Andrew the story of God parting the Red Sea after the Israelites left Egypt. Amazed at God's power, whenever he sees something people can't do, Andrew knows that "God can!"

"We can't make it rain but God can! We can't part the water but God can! God can do anything," says Andrew.

"Oh, Lord, you're great and groovy!" a six year old said during our praise time in children's church. His wonder about God was contagious. Another child chimed in.

"God, you made the rain and snow! You are awesome!" exclaimed Marcy, a bright redhead. To these and other kids, all things are possible for God.

CULTIVATING THE WONDER

How can you stir up this kind of wonder in your children? And how can you lead them from wonder to worship? It starts with our own response to God's world around us.

Has your child ever called you outside to see a rainbow or yelled, "Mom! Dad! You've gotta see this weird bug!" or "Come look at the lightning! It's streaking everywhere across the sky!" When we share in these moments and point kids to the Creator who made the great things they're seeing, we're actually fanning the flame of wonder—and helping them experience an important aspect of prayer. Wonder often precedes worship. When we don't stop and gaze with our children, we miss an opportunity to guide them (and ourselves) from wonder to praise.

A busy mom of five sons discovered this for herself when one of the boys called, "Mom, ya just gotta come out and see this sunset!" or "Come look at the huge wall cloud!" Phama often answered, "Just a minute!" or "I'm busy; I'll be there as soon as I get the dishes done." But when she finished her work and joined her son ten minutes later, the gorgeous colors had disappeared into the night.

Spontaneous moments of wonder are fleeting. The sunset quickly fades, snowflakes melt, lightning and rain stops, and life quickly retreats to business-as-usual. After missing several "wonders" and seeing the disappointment on her sons' faces, Phama finally realized that "Just a minute" or "I'm busy" throws cold water on her kids' wonder.

She resolved to stop her busyness and respond to their calls of "Come see this!"

Now Phama joins her sons in their moments of joy. Some of their "treasures" are creepy-crawly things like bugs, worms, and frogs. An adult may draw back from these "critters," but to young and curious eyes they are truly amazing creations. On the other hand, the boys also point out the first pink bud on her rose bush. Rushing by with bags of groceries, Phama might miss the delicate beauty, so she's now thankful for her sons' wonder-filled vision.

One early winter day Phama discovered her youngest child, one-year-old Zack, on the floor of the entry hall, tummy down, face pressed to the glass door, entranced by white snowflakes floating down from the sky—the first snowflakes he'd seen in his short life. Learning from past experiences, this wise mom didn't interrupt the moment. She watched as he fully enjoyed it.

When Zack got up a few minutes later, they talked. "Isn't God good that He would give us this picture, these beautiful snowflakes falling outside?" she asked her small son. With those brief words she pointed Zack to God, moving him from wonder to worship. Even a one year old can recognize wonder!

A SENSE OF ASTONISHMENT

The first step to moving our kids from wonder to worship is regaining our own sense of astonishment at God's creation and His working in our lives. I like what Alan Wright says about God's desire for us in *A Chance at Childhood Again:*

> The Heavenly Father wants His children to live in astonishment. Though He has offered us deep intimacy with Him and has welcomed us into the throne room itself, we must never lose our astonishment at His eternal majesty. We cannot know God except through the childlike eyes of astonishment.[4]

But maybe you're also an adult who has responded, "Later!" to kids' discoveries. Perhaps on the journey to adulthood your sense of wonder faded and was replaced by practicality, rationalism, busyness, and preoccupation with work and worry. I admit it: Mine did. As I got busier with each child and responsibility, juggling writing deadlines and the kids' school activities, supervising homework and helping in my husband's business, I missed many of the magical, miraculous things God put in my line of vision. I wanted to share in my kids' joy and sense of discovery, but there was so much to do.

Finally, frustrated, I asked the Lord, "What can I do?"

The Lord seemed to say, "Go fly a kite."

That seems so impractical, I thought.

"That's just the point," He answered.

So I purchased a kite for the children (and me) to fly. The kids enjoyed the challenge of getting the kite up in the air, but after a few minutes they ran off to swing and slide, leaving me holding the string. As the big red, yellow, and black kite caught the wind and flew higher and higher, my spirit soared too. After that afternoon, I was hooked on kites! Now I keep one in the trunk of the car for spontaneous flights.

Whenever I fly a kite in the field behind our house, at a nearby lake, or (if I'm really fortunate) at the beach, I can appreciate God's handiwork—the birds flying overhead, the blue sky, a puffy cascade of clouds—instead of focusing on my own earthly problems. Kite flying has stirred my sense of wonder and refreshed my spirit. It's also pointed me upward, toward God. I've learned that to cultivate a child's sense of wonder, we must first recultivate it within ourselves.

If kite flying is not your style, discover what makes your spirit soar. "My heart leaps up when I behold a rainbow in the sky. So was it when I was a child, so be it when I am a man, or let me die," wrote Wordsworth in "The Rainbow."[5] What makes your heart leap up? If it's flowers, go to a rose garden; if it's painting, head for an art museum. If it's music, put on a Mozart CD or praise tape and fill your heart with song. Take a walk and play on the swings with your toddler at the park. If you love stargazing, lay on the grass on summer nights with your kids and name the constellations or count stars. You could share with your child, "Isn't it amazing? God set every star in its place and named every one of them!" (Psalm 147:4).

When Jesus turned the water into wine, healed the blind and demon-possessed, and performed other miracles in His earthly ministry, some marveled and rejoiced while others scoffed. Some stood in awe of His power; others criticized Him or didn't even notice. I believe God wants us to be among the folks who don't take "little things" like sunrises and butterflies, friendship and quick recoveries, for granted, but who are filled with wonder and praise at His glory and goodness to us. Remember, when we cease to wonder, we cease to worship.

A Prayer for Wonder

Lord, it's easy for me to get busy
and miss the great things You do—
the way You fill the air with the music of birds singing
and fill the heavens with Your glory.
Help me to find wonder again
and to share in my children's wonder.
Let our awareness of the marvelous things
You've created and done in the world
lead us to worship You.
In Jesus' name, Amen.

HELPING KIDS PRAY

As you regain your sense of awe, here are some ways you can gently lead your child from his natural wonder to worship. Or, you can help revive wonder in an older child if he's grown "ho-hum" about the world around him.

- Say plenty of "Wow!" prayers. "Wow! prayers are the way we say to God, 'This thing I just saw or felt or smelled is terrific and beautiful, wonderful and awesome. I am saying this prayer so You know that I know…that You had something to do with this! Keep up the good work!'" explains Rabbi Marc Gellman, author of *How Do You Spell God?* Gellman adds: "If you go through life and never say 'Wow!' you better slow down or speed up or do something to get yourself to see all the Wow! that is in heaven and the earth all around you."[6]

    When I sat by Lake Leman in Switzerland, looking up at the snow-capped Alps that seemed to rise out of the lake, I sang a song, "Mountains bow down and the seas they roar at the sound of Your name." That was a "Wow!" prayer. David, who seemed to be perpetually amazed at God's wonders, said these kinds of prayers in the Psalms. (See Psalm 104, 139, and 148.)

- Give God the credit. You can take advantage of natural opportunities when your child is astonished by something—the Big Dipper on a clear night, a cluster of monarch butterflies, or waves crashing against the shore at a beach. You can slow down, look, listen, and give God credit for His beautiful creations. For example:

"Isn't God good to make those stars?"

"God made the honeysuckle for you to smell and enjoy. Doesn't it smell terrific? God is so good to give us little blessings like this to brighten our day."

"Isn't it great how God made you? The Bible says you are 'fearfully and wonderfully made.' You're His original handiwork! Let's thank Him" (Psalm 139).

- Take advantage of teachable moments. When you're outside together and hear the wind rustling the leaves, talk about how even the leaves praise God. Use the seasons and cycles of weather, animals at the zoo, and the variety of trees and flowers to discuss the God who created all things, and how His creation expresses His love and goodness.

- Try camping! Whether it's in a state park or even in the backyard, camping offers chances to revel in outdoor wonders. When your children ask questions about nature, instead of telling them your opinions and answers, ask, "What do you see? What do you hear?" Curiosity is key to maintaining a wide-eyed wonder about life.

- Notice and thank God for His work. Bedtime prayer is a good opportunity to review the day and appreciate the ways God provided for your (and your children's) needs or sent help when you most needed it. If your vision of God's goodness has clouded, ask Him to open your eyes to see His fingerprints on your life even in the midst of adversity and problems. Then share your gratefulness with your kids.

- Read God's Word with expectation, praying along with the psalmist, "Open my eyes that I may see wonderful things in your law" (Psalm 119:18). Charles Spurgeon said there are mysteries and treasures in the word which we haven't fully seen: "The Scriptures teem with marvels; the Bible is wonder-land: it not only relates miracles, but it is itself a world of wonders."[7]

- Look for the miraculous in everyday life: the miracle of a sunrise; the tiny, perfectly formed hands of a new baby; the colors of a rainbow. Whatever simple pleasure you find in nature or the world around you, let your heart leap up and enjoy it. And when your kids share some terrific thing with you, be it a green fuzzy insect or a gleaming rainbow, you'll be able to stop and appreciate it with them.

CHAPTER EIGHT

Beyond the Clattering Culture

God never ceases to speak to us,
but the noise of the world without
and the tumult of our passions within
bewilder us and prevent us from listening to Him.

FRANCOIS FÉNÉLON

For adults as well as children, time with God in prayer anchors us in the storms that hit from time to time. It's a session with the Counselor who listens to our pain and the Comforter who heals our hearts. Prayer is also the key to a close relationship with the Good Shepherd, who guides us along His path. It is the answer to most of our longings.

But if prayer should be our *first* resource, why is it sometimes our *last* resort—at the bottom of our priority list, edged in after school, work, sports, homework, meetings, eating, and television? Why is prayer relegated to being our spare tire instead of the steering wheel? And if we want our children to pray, why is it so hard to spend time interceding with them? Perhaps for the same reason there's so much power when we *do* pray. If Satan can't frustrate us any other way, he'll keep us frantically busy in order to squeeze prayer away from the center of our lives.

"The one concern of the devil is to keep the saints from prayer," writes Samuel Chadwick.[1] "He fears nothing from prayerless studies, prayerless work, prayerless religion [and I would add prayerless homes]. He laughs at our toil, mocks at our wisdom, but trembles when we pray."

GOING TOO FAST

Part of the problem of prayerlessness is that we live in a culture that moves in fast-forward. "We're fried by work, frazzled by the lack of time. Technology hasn't made our lives better, just busier. No wonder one quarter of us say we're exhausted. We need to chill out before we hit the breaking point," declared a recent *Newsweek* article.[2]

Most of us move at a more rapid pace than we want, driven not just by time urgencies but also by computer technologies, which are based on the nanosecond—an increment of one billionth of a second. In sharp contrast, prayer takes time; it demands slowing down long enough to dwell in God's presence.

Prayer also needs quietness—a hard commodity to come by! "We are usually surrounded by so much outer noise that it is hard to truly hear our God when He is speaking to us," says author Henri Nouwen.[3] "We have often become deaf, unable to know when God calls us and unable to understand in which direction He calls us." If adults struggle with hearing God in the midst of our clattering, high-speed culture, think about our children! They live in a media-barraged world that overblitzes their minds with TV, video, and blaring stereo noise. They race from school to after-school sports to Scouts, then eat at a local fast-food establishment for dinner and rush to do homework. Add time with friends, weekend sports or get-togethers, and church activities and the question becomes, "Where did the week go?"

SLOWING DOWN FOR PRAYER

When Vicki and Jeff Yinger's three children were young, their family got caught up in the "keep up with the Jones's" mentality. For the kids that collectively meant soccer, T-ball, basketball, dance and piano lessons, and a full range of children's ministry programs at church. Vicki also volunteered at the school and taught Bible studies. It became difficult to eat dinner together at night or pray with the kids. Family time dwindled and everybody was stressed out.

Consequently, when the family moved to a nearby community, Vicki and Jeff decided to make some changes—starting with limiting the activities and sports their kids were involved in. "Our philosophy is that kids need to play, and time after school is meant for play—

unstructured for the most part so they can make their own fun and use their imaginations," Vicki says.

The children, now thirteen, ten, and eight, played some organized sports but weren't driven to sign up every season. They had dinner together every night and plenty of conversation.

They also discovered time to regularly visit Geneva, a ninety-year-old family friend in a local nursing home. "When she was feeling bad, each of the kids would put a hand on Geneva and pray for her," remembers Vicki. The kids also got involved in their parents' home group ministry.

As a result, the Yinger children have been happier and less stressed. They enjoy their siblings more and even hang out together. The kids invite school and church friends to their house to play or for sleepovers, and their parents ask other families to join them for outings.

Slowing down also opened up windows of time to pray together, unhurriedly, at bedtime. After the kids say prayers like, "Lord, help Lex the dog not lick her infected paw; help us have a good day tomorrow," Vicki puts her hand on each of their hearts and asks, "Now what's God saying to your heart? What's the Holy Spirit speaking to your spirit? Is He prompting you to pray about something or to forgive someone?" Vicki finds that asking these questions helps her kids stay tender toward God and learn to listen to Him.

One night Luke, then nine, woke up from a vivid dream in which he sat in a rescue boat that hit a giant rock and exploded. The people inside the boat exploded too, and a bright light burst out of them. Luke climbed into bed with his parents, scared and upset because he had died in the dream too.

Vicki wrapped her arms around her son and prayed. After a few minutes of waiting on God, she felt prompted to ask, "Luke, is there anybody in your life you're holding a grudge against?" He immediately talked about how angry he'd been at his little sister, Claire. He asked God for forgiveness and for love for his sister. As they talked later, Luke and his mom realized the dream may have symbolized what happens when we don't repent of resentment and how the bitterness leads to destruction.

For this family, tender encounters with God and each other occur more frequently because the parents cleared their schedules, stopped the hectic pace, and took the time to be a family again.

POPCORN PRAISES AND PETITIONS

Slowing down is a step in the right direction for many of us. But maybe you're thinking, *That's great for this family, but we can't make those kinds of changes. We can't move, and we're already committed to too many activities we can't back out of right now.*

Even before you slow down, you can begin to pray "popcorn praises and petitions." These are brief, sincere, heartfelt requests and praises like, "What a rainbow, Lord!" or "Lord, please help me in this test,"or "God, what should I do?" Want a biblical model? How about when Peter began sinking at sea? "Lord, save me!" he cried (Matthew 14:30).

When my friend Barbara and her two sons drive to school or baseball games, work together in the backyard, or see something beautiful, they pray, "Thank you, God, for the sparkling sunlight on the lake (or bright fall leaves or yellow daffodils in that field)!" If they're at the zoo enjoying the vast variety of animals—the cheetah, giraffe, hippo, and flamingo—they praise God for His creativity: "Lord, only You could have designed the giraffe's long, skinny legs, the huge, funny-looking hippo and the beautiful coral color of the flamingo!"

If Barbara knows her husband, Allen, faces a stressful day, they send up "Lord, help Dad" prayers, asking for God to give him special wisdom and guidance. Or seven-year-old Dylan might pray, "Let Daddy's heart and mind stay at peace, Jesus."

This family directs popcorn prayers heavenward from morning till night, so staying in communication with God becomes as natural as talking with each other. No matter how busy they might be, they're centered in prayer. They're following Paul's advice to "pray always" (Ephesians 6:18).

It's amazing how kids pick up a prayerful attitude and imitate what they've seen and heard. When Fawn Parish's son, Joel, was three, whenever they passed a certain church he would pray, "Help the people to love You more. God bless Pastor Goldstein." (It didn't matter that the pastor's name was "Golden." God knew who little Joel was praying for!) Joel was following his mom's practice of letting everyday life become a visual aid for open-eyed, ongoing prayer.

Joy, a young mother of preschoolers, keeps prayer an "open book" before her children, expressing her gratitude to God but also admitting when she needs His help. "Since our example is the best teacher, my children see me cry out to God for help with my attitude and for patience when we hit rough spots during the day," Joy says. "They see me rejoice and thank Him for parking spaces and even when a recipe turns out. We thank God often for little things."

For Joy, devotion to God is a *lifestyle,* not just a rote exercise each morning. She prays with her kids in the grocery store and the doctor's office, and they're delighted when God divinely answers their simple requests.

When her two oldest boys were ages five and two, Joy stood with them in their bare backyard. "Let's ask God to provide a swing set," she suggested, concerned that her sons had no place to play. The preschoolers knelt with her on the grass and nodded their heads in agreement when Mom said, "Lord, it seems like we need a swing set back here. Would You just provide it so we can have fun in our backyard?"

There was no room in the budget for buying a swing set, so they left the need with God. Six months later Joy's father and his wife bought a larger home. He called to say, "There's a huge swing set in our new yard. It's real sturdy. If you'll come get it, your kids can have it."

When the swing set was set up in the backyard, Joy reminded her children, "Remember the day we prayed for a swing set? Look what God provided!" Some happy, spontaneous popcorn praises ascended from the backyard that day as the kids jumped onto the swings and played all afternoon.

A FAMILY BREAKFAST CLUB

Keeping in touch with God works better when we start each day with Him. "Although we want to make all our time, time for God, we will never succeed if we do not reserve a minute, an hour, a morning, a day, a week, a month, or whatever period of time for God and Him alone," writes Henri Nouwen.[4]

When Sandy's four children were in first, second, third, and fourth grades in California public schools, all were busy with work, school, household, and church responsibilities. But they still didn't want to lose touch with God or each other, so Sandy formed the Breakfast Club, her way of reserving time for God. She gave each family member a blank book for prayer requests and Bible study. She also provided crayons, colorful stickers, and markers. Each morning the family sat at the dining table with their breakfast and materials. The meeting began with a brief Bible reading while the kids ate. Then Mom and Dad took time to pray for each child, for his or her teachers, and for any possible problems in their classes that day.

The children enjoyed writing prayer requests in their books, keeping track of answered prayers, and the freedom to draw and decorate their prayer books as they talked and prayed. Breakfast Club lasted twenty to thirty minutes on busy days, but sometimes stretched to an hour on other days.

The Breakfast Club also provided the family a chance to pray for other people's needs: the teacher who hurt her back and had been yelling at her class; the boy who'd had a fight on the playground; the classmate hurting because her parent had divorced again. When the family heard about a young boy in Canada who was waiting desperately for a heart transplant, the children prayed for him each morning. Within a week he received a new heart. The children wrote to the boy and prayed for him during his recovery and return to school.

PRACTICING GOD'S PRESENCE

Perhaps without realizing it, these moms were passing on to their children a sense of the heavenly Father's presence. Jesus practiced the presence of God whether on a hillside ministering to thousands, in the temple delivering a message, healing someone at poolside, or teaching the disciples. Brother Lawrence of the seventeenth century echoed this way of living in his classic collection of letters and notes, *The Practice of the Presence of God.* No matter how mundane or long the task, Brother Lawrence nurtured a habitual sense of God's presence.[5]

"Practicing the presence" is also possible today. Mother Teresa, for example, integrated God into her busy ministry to the street people of Calcutta instead of fragmenting the day into "spiritual" and "real life" compartments. As we cultivate an awareness of God's presence, all of life becomes a prayer. Mother Teresa expressed it well:

> There are some people who, in order not to pray, use as an excuse the fact that life is so hectic that it prevents them from praying.

This cannot be.

Prayer does not demand that we interrupt our work, but that we continue working as if it were a prayer...What matters is being with Him, living in Him, in His will. To love with a pure heart, to love everybody, especially to love the poor, is a twenty-four-hour prayer.[6]

Although she worked tirelessly serving the poor and ministering to others, Mother Teresa lived the moments of her days in constant communion with Him. What an honor it is to practice His presence, no matter how busy our lives may be, and pass this attitude on to our children.

A Prayer for a Quiet Heart

Heavenly Father,
I want prayer to be my family's steering wheel and first resource,
not our spare tire and last resort.
Forgive me for prayerlessness in my own life,
for letting the clattering culture around me
dictate my priorities and drown out Your voice.
Quiet my racing heart so I can be aware of Your presence
and hear Your voice throughout all the hours of the day.
Let all of my life be a prayer.
In Jesus' name, Amen.

HELPING KIDS PRAY

If we're going to help our children get beyond the clattering culture and learn to pray, they do need quiet times. Here are suggestions to help them find a quiet place in their souls.

- Quiet the bouncing ball. As you begin a prayer time, help children quiet down by comparing the scattered thoughts that jump around in their heads to a bouncing ball. For some kids the ball bounces fast, which makes it harder to settle down; for others the ball moves slowly. Then light a candle and turn down the lights, encouraging the kids to focus on God for a few minutes. Turn on peaceful instrumental praise music and ask them to close their eyes for thirty to sixty seconds, as they "slow down the bouncing ball." Ask them to picture Jesus in their mind's eye for awhile because they'll be talking to Him. Before they pray, the children can open their eyes and talk about what they experienced when the bouncing ball settled down. Proceed to pray for the needs at hand.[7]

• Find a time and place apart. Create a special place in your home for quiet time with God. For example, a pillow to kneel on and a night light in the corner of your child's bedroom, or a special chair in the family room or patio.

• Limit television time. In a recent newsletter article titled "The Conspiracy of Interruptions," pastor David Wilkerson describes one of the greatest conspiracies the enemy uses to keep families from prayer—the television. He suggests that the still, small voice of God has become "drowned out by all the worldly voices emanating from the tube" and points out that by the time a teenager reaches age eighteen, he's watched six years of TV but has spent only four months in church. When we spend hours and weeks listening to the clamoring voices of the world, a lot of time is consumed—time we could be hearing the Lord in prayer.[8]

Limiting the amount of time you and your children watch television not only enhances prayer, but also opens space for family reading, hobbies, hospitality, and other activities, including homework that isn't rushed through before the next sit-com.

The idea of limiting television may sound radical, but a diet of wisely chosen programs—where it becomes the occasional dessert rather than the main course of your children's lives—can work wonders for their spiritual life.

CHAPTER NINE

The Joy of Servant Prayers

Children are God's messengers,
day by day sent forth
to share His love, and hope, and peace.

AUTHOR UNKNOWN

Dear God, help me to have a good day at school. Please bless Mommy and Daddy and my dog Snickers. And help me and Sara to get along and not fight."

"Lord, help us to have a fun time on our trip, and nobody get sick in the car."

"Dear God, I need a friend. I don't have anyone to play with on the playground. And could we go to MacDonald's for dinner?"

"Jesus, could you send me a puppy? And change Dad's mind so he'll let me keep it!"

Do these prayers sound familiar? They do to me. My children prayed a lot of "help us to have a good day" prayers.

It's normal for children's requests to center around their own needs and family. Kids are born "totally egocentric," says educator Karyn Henley.[1] The world revolves around them. Even their parents seem to be an extension of themselves. Preschoolers especially are in the "ME" stage. Everything is "mine!" Convincing them to share one of their toys with a neighbor child is a challenge.

However, by the time kids reach the school years, their world widens a little. Prayers for puppies, pizza, and good days continue, but we can gently move children beyond themselves to develop a concern and compassion for others. We can help them pray "servant prayers" instead of just making self-centered requests.

Just as with anything else, we start with baby steps—praying for their needs, then expanding to caring about people in their immediate circle of family and friends, and later interceding for people in a larger venue, such as those living in another country.

Sandy Koop, a fifth grade teacher at a Michigan Christian school, uses her trifocal glasses to demonstrate the widening circles of prayer. She explains that the lower part of her lens is for reading up close. This close-up vision is like praying for our needs and for those of friends and family, the people we interact with regularly. The next trifocal lens enables her to see within a twelve-foot range, and it represents people she hears about at church, school, or in the community. The top part of the trifocal lens is for distance vision, and represents our prayers for people we may never meet this side of heaven—government leaders, unevangelized people groups, or missionaries in a foreign country.

My husband, Holmes, and I helped to broaden our children's prayer circle by involving them in intercession for members of our extended family. We also took them along to pray if a friend checked into the hospital or a family member was ill. One Saturday morning when Justin, Chris, and Alison were three, five, and eight, I woke up after a vivid dream. In my dream "Grandpo," the children's great-grandfather, was going blind and we needed to take the children to visit him while he could still see.

I shared the dream with my husband and told him of the urgency I felt about taking the children to see Grandpo. So we put aside our Saturday plans, called Holmes's grandparents, and packed up the kids for a day trip to Kansas. Although I had no prior knowledge of any problems, I sensed that we needed to pray for Grandpo's eyes. Fortunately, Holmes didn't think I was crazy and agreed to pray with me for his granddad.

After we arrived and chatted over fresh angel food cake and milk, we told Grandpo and Grandmo that we wanted to pray for his eyes, if that was okay. Although prayer for healing was unfamiliar to them, they said our visit might be God's timing. The next Monday Grandpo was scheduled for laser surgery on his right eye. He had a bleeding retina, and if it was left unchecked he'd lose his sight in that eye. The doctor hadn't given Grandpo much hope that this procedure would work, but felt it was at least worth a try.

The children, Holmes and I gathered around Grandpo, placed our hands on him, and prayed for healing, for wisdom and skill for the doctor, and for Grandpo's sight to be preserved. Then we spent the rest of the day eating, playing outside with the kids, and chatting on the porch before the long drive back to Oklahoma City.

On Monday Grandpo's eye surgery went smoothly and within a few days his vision cleared. We were encouraged and the episode boosted our children's faith. They saw us care enough to change our plans and drive five hours to pray for their great-grandfather, all on a chance that perhaps God was speaking through my dream.

On our next visit to Holmes's grandparents they showed us a letter from the doctor, who expressed surprise at how successfully the laser procedure had restored Grandpo's sight. (Doctors had estimated only a 10 percent chance of improvement.) We all rejoiced. The kids' circle of prayer widened and they continued to pray for their great-grandfather.

FROM "BOOBOO PRAYERS" TO AMBULANCE SIRENS
Moving our kids toward servant prayers can be as simple as noticing people in trouble.

When her boys were young, in place of a "Booboo Bunny" (a soft, terry cloth rabbit ice pack), Patty prayed for their scraped knees and bumps. Grant and Andrew, her preschoolers, usually stopped crying because the prayer took their attention off the "booboo." This pattern helped the boys develop caring hearts toward others with "booboos." When Andrew fell down, Grant said, "Mommy, let's pray for Andrew." When Mom burned her finger, four-year-old Andrew bowed his head and said, "Please, Jesus, help Mommy's finger and take away the pain."

Then Patty widened their circle of concern to those outside the family. Whenever they heard a medical emergency siren or encountered an accident on the road, she prayed aloud and asked her sons to join in. When an ambulance sped victims toward the hospital, in her mind's eye she pictured Jesus rushing to those people on the wings of their prayers, ready to heal and comfort. Then she shared this image with her boys.

As a result, Patty's sons grew in compassion for others. Now when they see a person who doesn't have a coat, they pray for him. When they pass a homeless person, they ask their mom to buy a sack of food for him. When they hear about people who are sick, *they* remind *her* to pray for them. And when Grant went to Christian-school kindergarten, he took his practice of praying for ambulances to school and shared it with his teacher. Now the class of twenty-five children stops and prays whenever they hear a siren.

From seeds like these, God can grow tender hearted kids who pray for others.

A number of years ago Beth Thomas suffered serious head injuries in a car accident. After being rushed to the hospital in an ambulance, she lay comatose in the intensive care unit for thirty-six hours. Her stay in the hospital lasted three weeks. Consequently, she and her husband are particularly sensitive to car accidents and, whenever they hear sirens, they pray for the victims. When their daughter grew old enough to understand and participate, she became a part of their "Emergency Prayer Team."

"Emily, I'm driving and need to pay attention," her mom said if they were on the road and an ambulance sped by. "Would you pray for this person and the family who is going to get the news? And for the doctors who are going to take care of them in the ER?"

For Emily, now thirteen, interceding for accident victims is as natural as praying for two young friends with disabilities who have endured numerous surgeries, or for an unchurched girl in the neighborhood.

When Emily was eight years old, her mom began using *You Can Change the World*[2] in their nightly devotions. In this marvelous book, each letter of the alphabet focuses on one of world's unreached people groups—from Azeris to Zulus—and includes a story of a child from each country or group, full-color illustrations, maps, and information about the child's religion and culture. It also provides seven short, simple prayers kids can say for the child and country. Reading the book together, and explaining to Emily that Jesus loves all children, helped Emily realize she could spread His love by praying for kids in other countries. Emily caught a vision for the world.

One church used *You Can Change the World, Volumes I and II*, over a two-year period in the elementary Sunday school classes. Twice a month the teacher read about one of the unreached people groups or countries and the children prayed for them. Helping the children be more mission-minded only took a brief amount of time, but it opened up a world of intercession for them. For older children, the *Global Prayer Digest*[3] is a good prayer resource. Each day focuses on a different unreached people group and includes a short story and prayer suggestions. Likewise, *Operation World*[4] effectively guides teens through prayer by providing statistics, detailed maps, and vital information about each country.

In many of these countries, the spiritual and physical needs are urgent. According to World Vision International, approximately two billion of the world's children, eighteen years and younger, are "at risk." They suffer from poverty, hunger, child labor, prostitution, or other abuse.[5] These kids need prayer! That's why the Caleb Project, Wycliffe, Youth With a Mission's Kings Kids, Esther International, and other Christian organizations sponsor special days of prayer and resources for kids in crisis. For example, young pray-ers can join the Worldwide Day of Prayer for Children at Risk and use resources like the *Children's 30-Day Muslim Prayer Guide, Children of the Window Prayer Calendar,* and the book, *From Arapesh to Zuni, A Book of Bibleless People*. These resources convince kids that when they pray, it makes a difference worldwide.

"PRAYER WALKING" IN THE BUILDING

Kids especially assimilate a country's prayer needs if they can see, taste, touch, and hear about that nation's culture. Prayer walking—without leaving the building—furnishes a sensory motivation for kids to get excited and pray.

One year Pete Hohmann, children's minister at Mechanicsville Christian Center in Mechanicsville, Virginia, took about sixty kids from grades one to six on a "prayer walk" to eight cities around the world. Each of eight rooms in the church building represented a major city that is unreached by the gospel. Before the prayer journey began, Pete taught about conversational prayer, divided the kids into groups, and encouraged them to pray for each "city" as they passed through it.

Entering the rooms, the children learned facts about the cities and their cultures. They sampled rice dishes from Casablanca, listened to Japanese music, and viewed a video on the slums of Calcutta. They learned a Hebrew song from Jerusalem and how to pray Muslim-style, wiping the blessings on their faces with their hands.

After each group completed their journey around the cities, the children gathered in the main meeting room for sharing and debriefing. One ten-year-old boy drew a picture of the 10/40 window, the regions stretching from North Africa to Japan, where the majority of the world's unreached people live. Over the window the little boy drew God's hand releasing blessings, like rain, on these countries. Another child was struck by the fact that in one city there was only one believer for every hundred people. She drew a stick figure surrounded by ninety-nine others to depict the huge need for prayer.

Children cheered and clapped as the artists explained their pictures. They yelled, "Lord, send the light!" as Pete called out the name of each city. And they learned that they can impact the world when they pray, even in places thousands of miles across the earth.[6]

PRAYING IN THE CLASSROOM

Christian school teachers and home school parents can impart a world vision to their students by integrating prayer into classroom activities. Sharron Shaw, a second grade teacher in Dallas, Texas, mobilized her students to pray for their principal. His birthday was November 1, so on the first of each month they prayed for his requests and needs. As the principal shared how God had answered their prayers, the students were motivated to pray for bigger things.

Sandy Koop, the teacher who explained "trifocal praying" to her fifth graders, develops her students' vision further by inviting international students from a nearby university to talk with the class. They've had visitors from Thailand, China, Pakistan, and other countries. Once she presented a unit on Islam, and when the students saw country after country with fewer than one percent Christians, they declared, "We need to pray for more missionaries to the Muslims!"

Several months later a missionary from Northern Iraq, who worked among the Kurds, visited their classroom. As they listened to her stories, students felt God was answering their prayers. As she traveled back to Iraq, the children continued to pray for her and the Kurdish people.

Sandy's class also participated in the "Adopt a Leader" program through the Michigan Family Forum. In this program students and prayer groups adopted a state leader to pray for during the school year. Then on the National Day of Prayer, they traveled to the state capitol and met the leaders in person. She and her students also pray for world leaders when crises arise—and in the process, these ten year olds are developing a heart for the world and feel personally involved in current events through their prayers.[7]

They're beginning to experience the joy of servant prayer.

A Prayer for Compassion

Lord, I often have tunnel vision
and am focused on my problems
and my family's concerns.
Yet I want my children to have a heart for others
and pray with compassion.
So, Lord, please expand our hearts and fill them
with Your love for all people,
people of different countries, races, and colors.
Open our eyes to the needs of others
and widen our circle of prayer.
In Jesus' name, Amen.

HELPING KIDS PRAY

Whoever is in your circle—family, friends, missionaries, students, pastors, principals, and teachers, those with special needs or disabilities at church and school—embrace them in your children's prayer life. Then find one of the excellent resources mentioned in this chapter, or those at the end of this book, to help focus your child's attention. You'll significantly move him toward servant prayers. Also try the following ideas:

- *Seize opportunities to pray.* If you are a home school or Christian school teacher or parent, you can integrate prayer into academic lessons. For example, when you study American history or government, pray for senators, congressmen, and leaders in Washington. When you study Middle Eastern countries, pray for the people in those nations. When you see news stories that alarm or sadden you or your children, turn that concern into prayers for the people involved.

- *Reach out to internationals.* Invite international students from local universities over for dinner and get to know them. Our friends, the Hooks, have invited many university students from other countries for meals with their kids. Their tablecloth contains the embroidered hand print and name of each of these students so the family can remember them in prayer.

- *Join with other Christians in the Worldwide Day of Prayer for Children at Risk.* Set aside the first Saturday in June each year to pray for children who are suffering around the world. For the *Seven-Day Prayer Guide,* prayer activities, and planning ideas for your family or prayer group, contact Viva Network, P.O. Box 633, Oxford, OX2 OXZ, U.K. You can also e-mail to prayer@viva.org or fax to 044-1865-203567.

The Power of God's Promises

*God never made a promise
that was too good to be true.*

D. L. MOODY

Excitement and anticipation filled the church's prayer room. Twenty-five teenagers had practiced their songs, skits, and testimonies for a nine-week evangelistic tour, and now they readied to leave. As the national King's Kids team formed a circle, they prayed, asking God about His will for their trip, and what specific Scriptures might direct their efforts.

During prayer several team members felt impressed with the same message: Success would occur through unity and loving one another. One young man felt God showed him specific verses in John 15:12–17, where Jesus explains the imperative of loving one another as the foundation of everything we do: "My command is this: Love each other as I have loved you. Greater love has no one than this, that one lay down his life for his friends."

As the teens prayed about these verses, they felt the key to successful ministry would be actively expressing their love by serving the international team (older young adults from different countries) that shared the stage with them. "Love one another" became the team's theme. Each of them prayed specifically, but privately, for someone on the international team every day.

Near the end of the nine weeks, the teenagers asked God how to say goodbye to the older team they'd grown to love. As they prayed and talked, the teens decided each was to wash the feet of the person they'd prayed for during the tour. Members of the international team were moved to tears as, one by one, they each had their feet washed by the young person who had been secretly praying for them throughout the tour.

In turn, the teens gained a fresh excitement over God's direction of their lives through Scripture and prayer. Looking back, they also realized that many people in the churches they visited had made decisions to follow Christ. God had blessed their obedience to His Word.

LETTING SCRIPTURE GUIDE OUR PRAYERS

Whenever we're unsure how to pray, Scripture can guide us. We can "pray God's Word," believing that what He has said is eternally true.

Have you ever read your Bible and it seemed as if God shined a flashlight on a special verse just so you would notice it? I remember the day I read 2 Timothy 1:7: "For God did not give us a spirit of timidity, but a spirit of power, of love and of self-discipline." I had read that verse before, but I was struggling with anxiety over our son's health problems and knew immediately that those words were for me. God didn't want me to be afraid when we rushed Justin to the emergency room; He didn't want me to worry about His next asthmatic episode. The Lord wanted me to trust Him with all my heart. *But how can I do that?* I thought.

I decided to agree with God's will in this matter. I wrote the date in the margin of my Bible and prayed that verse aloud: "Lord, You said in Your Word that You haven't given me a spirit of fear; You don't want me to be worried and anxious about Justin and his asthma attacks. So I pray for Your love and power to replace that fear. Let me be so filled with Your love that there won't be any room for anxiety or worry. In Jesus' name, Amen." Speaking to God in His own words calmed me. It gave me confidence and a new ability to handle my son's health problems.

As I look through the pages of my Bible, I find many of those dated passages with the initials of my children, husband, or another family member for whom I was praying a certain verse. Especially as I journeyed with Christ through the parenting years, the Bible became a vital resource in my prayer life. The Scriptures inspired my conversations with God, gave me direction, and revealed what to focus on in prayer.

For example, when I felt concerned for Justin during his stormy adolescence, I asked God to show me specific Scriptures to pray for him. He led me to the words Paul prayed for the new converts at Ephesus: "I pray for you constantly," wrote Paul, "asking God...to give you wisdom to see clearly and really understand who Christ is and all that he has done for you. I pray that your hearts will be flooded with light so that you can see something of the future he has called you to share...I pray that you will begin to understand how incredibly great his power is to help those who believe in him" (Ephesians 1:16–19, TLB).

What an awesome prayer! I repeated this and other prayers, personalizing them by putting my children's names in the verses.

"Lord, help my kids to fix their thoughts on what is true, and good and right and pure" (Philippians 4:8).

"Give Chris and Alison patience, steadiness, and encouragement; help them to live in harmony with us, their friends and each other with a Christlike attitude" (Romans 15:5).

"Lord, help Justin, Chris, and Alison to put You first today and to trust You with all their hearts instead of leaning on their own thinking or understanding of things. Assure them that You'll direct their steps and crown their efforts with success" (Proverbs 3:5–6).

I felt assured I was praying what the Lord desires for my children—and He loves them even more than I do! As I prayed God's Word back to Him, I was filled with faith instead of doubt. My confidence in God and His promises increased, and I trusted Him to fulfill the promises in His way and on His timetable. I not only saw Him work in the lives of our children, but my spiritual roots deepened too.

WHAT CAN I PRAY?

As I've talked to parents, some of their frustration about prayer centers on not knowing what to ask of God, feeling that somehow their words aren't "right." One dad said, "I wanted so much for my children. But when I knelt in prayer, I invariably found the same tired words rolling from my lips." Interestingly, it's one of the dilemmas that children express too. I've been told, "I don't know what to pray or how to pray besides 'Lord, bless this food to the nourishment of our bodies' like my dad prays or, 'Help me to have a good day.'" An even more common question from kids is, "What can I say to God in my daily quiet time so I'm not saying the same old thing every day?"

A solution to this dilemma is praying the Scriptures. You will be amazed at how much life it brings into your prayers and those of your children. Still, biblical praying isn't a formula or a magical method; it's simply letting the Bible guide your prayers. Since the Scriptures are God's words, you can't go wrong as you study and incorporate them into conversations with Him. When we pray God's Word, we know our prayers are right on target!

Heather, a sixth grader, had played the violin for two years. She wanted to improve and move up to a better seat in the orchestra, but progress eluded her. She had a poor relationship with her teacher and felt so discouraged she wanted to quit. Her mom suggested that instead, she keep playing and "pray Scripture" over the situation.

As Heather studied her Bible, two verses seemed to apply to her. She committed them to memory, praying them each day. The first was Psalm 5:12: "For surely, O LORD, you bless the righteous; you surround them with your favor as with a shield." Heather's second verse was Philippians 4:13: "I can do everything through him who gives me strength." Continuing to practice her lessons, she prayed for favor with her music teacher, and for strength to do her best.

By the spring semester of her eighth-grade year, Heather had moved up several chairs. And her music teacher surprised her by saying to the class, "If I were giving an award for the most improved student, it would go to Heather." She and the teacher had developed such a good relationship that, most days, Heather took her lunch to the orchestra room where they ate together.

OTHER BLESSINGS OF "PRAYING THE SCRIPTURES"
Scriptural praying will also help your kids by:

• *Jump-starting their prayer time.* Just like priming the pump spills water out of a well, praying from a Bible passage helps kids connect with God. Much like a salutation, "Dear Mom," moves them into the body of a letter to express what they want to say, praying words directly from the Bible initiates conversation with God. "Thank You, Lord! How good You are! Your love for us continues on forever." Or, "Lord; O Lord my God, how great You are! You are robed with honor and majesty and light!" (Psalms 106:1; 104:1, TLB).

You'll be surprised at how easily children can understand the importance of letting God's Word jump-start and guide our prayers. Hannah, a six year old I know, accompanied her mother and dad to their fellowship group meeting and drew pictures as the adults discussed their current struggles. One woman talked about how she had been in a "desert," and hadn't heard God speak to her in a long time. A few other adults chimed in that they too, wished God would speak to them more often.

Hannah listened. On the way home, she said to her mom, "Don't the grown-ups read their Bibles? God speaks to us every time we pick up our Bible and read it, because He wrote it! If they would just open their Bibles, Mom, I know they'd hear God talk to them."

• *Directing them toward what to pray.* The Bible is a gold mine of prayers. David's confessions to God, Jesus' prayers to His Father, Paul's petitions on behalf of young churches, and many other prayers set a pattern for kids to follow. They also guide children when they wonder, "What's God's will in this situation?" and help them pray for other people.

In a recent Bridge Builders' outreach, the children, aged five to twelve, prepared to enter an inner-city housing project to share songs, give testimonies, and do practical service. An eleven-year-old boy read from 1 Kings 18:26–29 about how the worshipers of Baal cried out to their gods for help but received no answer. He shared how the people in the housing project were also crying out to gods of drugs, alcohol, and money—gods that really couldn't help them.

"We have to tell them about the true God," he told his group, "because only He can help them." As Scripture guided the young people's prayers, they saw God work mightily that day in their outreach to the housing project.[1]

On many issues, God doesn't leave us to guess what His will is— He reveals His will throughout the pages of Scripture. There are promises concerning God's plans for children's lives, the provision He has available, the future and hope He keeps in store for those who trust Him. He provides direction for young people to hide His Word in their hearts so they won't sin against Him (Psalm 119:11) and how He'll give them courage to live without copying the behavior of the world (Romans 12:1–2). As they pray Scripture, kids grow in confidence because they know their prayers are in harmony with God's Word.

Judson Cornwall says, "There is no greater source of the expressed will of God than the Scriptures. As we bring them into our prayer lives, we are far more likely to pray according to the will of God than when we merely pray out of our minds and emotions."[2]

• *Giving kids a prayer vocabulary.* To write well, we need a wide vocabulary. To pray effectively, we need God's vocabulary. As young people grow in God's Word, they don't have to struggle for words about who God is and what to say to Him. Their praise vocabulary will grow as they discover He is their Rock, Shield, Victor, Sovereign and Promise-Keeper. They can express their feelings honestly to God as they become familiar with the Psalms, which depict the entire range of human emotions: joy, sadness, contentment, desperation, and a need for help. "Hear, O LORD, and answer me, for I am poor and needy" (Psalm 86:1). "In you, O LORD, I have taken refuge; let me never be put to shame" (Psalm 71:1).

Knowing God's Word can be a powerful strength to our children, a comfort in times when we can't be with them. Hannah discovered this when she and her grandmother were in a terrible car accident. When Hannah's mom, Wyndi, arrived on the scene shortly after the crash, Hannah stood in the road near the car, seemingly unharmed. Her mom, sobbing at the prospect that her mother's life was hanging by a thread, could barely recall basic information for the emergency personnel, but Hannah composed herself enough to answer questions.

Later, at the recommendation of counselors, Wyndi spoke to her daughter about what she was thinking at the scene of the accident. Hannah recalled that she was thinking of a Bible verse. "I recited John 3:16 over and over in my head," Hannah said.

Why didn't God help her recall that He is the God of all comfort? Wyndi puzzled. She asked Hannah why John 3:16 had helped her.

Hannah quoted the verse, then explained that following the impact, she had tried to wake her grandmother but couldn't. She thought Grandma was dead, but knew that she believed in Jesus. That verse assured her that if Grandma was dead then "she was already having eternal life."

Could there be any greater comfort than the assurance of salvation? Hannah's grandmother did recover, but in the process Wyndi saw first-hand how God revealed wisdom beyond her years to a nine year old through His Word.

As you incorporate scriptural praying into your daily life and show your children how to let God's Word guide their prayers, you'll be encouraged as they grow in love and relationship with their Heavenly Father.

A Prayer for Illumination

Dear Lord, thank You for the precious promises in Your Word,

the ideal prayer manual.

And thank You that as we pray, none of Your words return void,

but they accomplish what You planned.

Open my eyes to specific verses

You want me to pray for and with my children,

so Your Word can shape our prayers.

Thank You for hiding Your truth from those

who think themselves so wise

and for revealing it to little children!

In Jesus' name, Amen.

HELPING KIDS PRAY

Here are some ways your children can let God's Word and promises guide their prayers.

- Model praying the Scriptures. As you read the Bible look for the promises and plans God has for your kids. Let these verses shape your prayers. When a verse addresses what your child needs, write it down and date it. Then share the verse with your child. When children hear their parents pray Scripture, this becomes a natural way of praying for them too.

"God will give Scriptures for all our children if only we will take the time to ask Him," says author Quin Sherrer. "As each new year begins, I ask the Lord to direct me to the Scriptures He wants me to pray for my children in the coming year. I then write them in my prayer journal in January and refer to them throughout the year."[3] Great advice—but you don't have to wait for New Year's Day. You can start today, asking Him to direct you to specific verses to pray for your kids.

- Hide God's Word in their hearts. Find fun ways to memorize Scripture as a family so your children store up God's Word in their hearts. When kids know the Bible, the Holy Spirit can bring its truths to mind during prayer time. They can pray from a rich storehouse of wisdom.

  Try the step-by-step approach. Take a block or chapter of Scripture and memorize it with your children, just one verse a day. Then add to it, verse by verse, reciting what you've learned together at the breakfast table or bedtime. Before long your kids will recall an entire portion of Scripture from memory. There are many painless ways to put into practice the parenting advice in Deuteronomy 6:6–9, which tells us to bind His Word on our hearts, thoughts, and actions. Also, Christian bookstores sell creative methods for Scripture memory.

  When your children bring verses home from Sunday school, show them how to pray these back to God. For example, maybe your daughter has learned Isaiah 11:2 in class and carried the verse home, printed on construction paper. You can incorporate that verse into your morning prayer with her by saying, "Lord, may Your Spirit rest upon Ashley today at school—the Spirit of wisdom and of understanding, the Spirit of counsel and of power, the Spirit of knowledge and of the fear of the Lord."

  Or if there's a difficult child in your son's class at school, you can apply Matthew 5:44 and teach him how to turn it into a prayer: "Lord, help me to love my enemies and forgive this boy who picked on me—and even to pray for him."

- Help them grow in God's ways. Explain that to grow in God's ways, we agree with His Word, thank Him for His commands, and ask for His help to "walk them out" in our lives. Children can pray, "I thank You that You want me to live a godly life, that You want me to have wisdom; You want me to trust You with all my heart. Help me to do this, Lord" (Proverbs 3:5). When they read a passage that expresses God's will, encourage them to pray it with a simple, "Help me to do that, Lord." When kids turn verses into prayer, Scripture becomes alive and relevant.

- Use a word picture or analogy. Recently when sharing about praying Scripture in children's church, I said, "God's Word is a little like a two-party check. He has already signed it. When we pray it, we're signing it. And both parties have to sign the check for it to come to pass." [4]

    I also found an analogy they could relate to from Catherine Marshall's wonderful book *Adventures in Prayer*. She wrote:

    > The Scriptures are letters—personal letters from God to each one of us. If you want to open your mail, just read through any of the passages that begin with the word *whosoever*—and substitute the words "that means me" for *whosoever*. These are the promises God has made to each one of…And we can take God at His Word! [5]

- Respond when God speaks. Ask your children what they're hearing from God as they read Scripture or pray. "Are there any verses here that you think God might want us to pray about?" Or, "What Scripture verse has come to your mind as we've been praying?"

    When we take the time to ask children and take seriously what they share, it's a blessing to them and to us, for God loves to speak to and through children. In fact, Jesus said, "I praise you, Father, Lord of heaven and earth, because you have hidden these things from the wise and learned, and revealed them to little children. Yes, Father, for this was your good pleasure" (Matthew 11:25–26).

Dear God,
I pray that you will cleanse my hart, O God. I love You, God. I love Jesus too.
I love the Lord!

—*Drew, 8*

dear god
please forgive me for all my sins and please help anais in my class take her virus away. and protect the rest of our class not to catch the virus! and please help chad too. in jesus name. amen

—*Michelle, 10*

Lord, help us to remember
every child in the world
is our brother and sister
and they are hurting
so also we are hurting.

—*A child in Scotland*

CHAPTER ELEVEN

Different Kids, Different Bents

*Just as we need a diversity of gifts in the body,
different kinds of intercessors are required
to complete the whole ministry of intercession.
If we can understand and put these differences to work,
God will be blessed, the enemy crippled,
and the group united in powerful prayer.*

ALICE SMITH

The Rubottom children, in pajamas and slippers, quiet down as their parents descend the stairs to the family room to begin evening prayers. With eight children, each different from the other, it's an ongoing challenge for this mom and dad to keep these prayer times stimulating.

Emily, fifteen, nurtures a strong, growing relationship with the Lord and leans toward concise, to-the-point prayers. "I love to pray with other people in a group because it helps me feel closer to them and our great God," says Emily. Before she lays down to sleep, she kneels by her bed to stay awake and focus on the Lord.

Christopher, thirteen, is quiet, and when asked to pray, he shows little emotion. Yet he says appropriate and on-target prayers. He is a practical pray-er.

Hannah, twelve, utters compassionate, heartfelt prayers. Her sensitive conscience confesses quickly when she does anything wrong. She loves to talk to God in bed before falling asleep. For a time Hannah struggled with fear, but by memorizing and praying God's Word, she was released from this anxiety.

Abby, ten, and her sister Cammie, nine, are quiet when Dad asks, "Is there anything you have to pray about?" Lately they've been self-conscious and when asked if they'd like to pray aloud, the girls replied with a collective "No." But they draw messages to God in pictures and love to sing songs to Him.

The two younger children, Jonathan, seven, and Marianna, five, are just learning to pray aloud in family devotions. When Dad asks for prayer requests, Jonathan shares concerns for his neighborhood buddies and for friends back in Texas who had a death in the family. Marianna loves to sing praises, pray when asked, and talk about her love for Jesus.

The baby, Timothy, eighteen months, chimes in with "Amen!" when his siblings pray. Recently his mother overheard him praying in his crib about a new favorite food: "Dear Jesus, Pizza, please. Amen."

In another family I know, the children have invented their own ways to pray privately, in addition to family devotional times. The son sings praises and talks to God as he cuts the lawn or works outside on the farm. The daughters love to dance to praise music and choreograph their own worship. They also pray while lying in bed or curling up in a cozy wingback chair to write in their journals.

All of these young family members talk to God however it best suits them. Essentially, this is the key to turning our kids into interested and satisfied pray-ers. When we throw out the cookie cutter and allow children to approach God according to their individual personalities and natural bents, they enjoy their communication with Him.

WIRED DIFFERENTLY

God created each of us to be one-of-a-kind. Though we differ in design, we are wonderfully made. He created us specifically for His purposes, for the things He planned us to be and do. Practically speaking, we're each "wired" in a special way. This wiring affects our learning styles, spiritual gifts, and how we pray and experience God's presence.

Some of us are "Listeners and Talkers." We're people with verbal and auditory strengths who like to listen to sermons and seminars, but most of all, love to talk. We learn best by asking questions and discussing ideas, and we enjoy praying in groups. Jessica, a teenager I know, is wired this way. She gets more out of the Bible if she reads it aloud. She loves meeting weekly with her girls' study and prayer group, and finds she can focus her thoughts in prayer best if she talks to God out loud rather than silently. Jess particularly delights in praying for other people and hearing how God answers.

Others of us are "Movers and Doers," energetic folks who learn best through movement and a hands-on approach. David, an eleven year old, is this type of learner. He understands a lot more about electricity if he conducts several experiments before reading or completing a worksheet about it. Through the actual process of doing—touching, trying things out and seeing for himself how things work—concepts become clearer and the "light bulb" inside his head switches on.

David is also very sports-oriented and plays hockey. He finds that games are a meaningful place for him to connect with God. In one game, he was involved in a "shoot-out." The game was tied and the starting five players of each team had to take a shot on goal until some-one scored. The pressure was on. David's mom watched from the stands, praying for him because he sometimes struggles as a defensive player and isn't one of the team's stars. Before he took his shot, David raised his head to the ceiling for a long time. Then he skated down the rink and scored, winning the game for his team.

"David, when you looked up, what were you doing?" his mom asked him later.

"It was a Mighty Duck moment," David answered, "and I prayed because this was real life. I said, 'God, You know this is a want, not a need, but please answer my want and help me score!'"

Movers like David may sense God's presence best when jogging, hiking, riding a bike, or participating in other types of physical exercise or "real life" action better than when they're sitting still.

Then there are the "Lookers" with visual and spatial strengths, who learn best by reading, observing, and "painting pictures" in their minds. They are often more quiet, even silent, pray-ers who may be gifted as artists and communicate their praise and love for God through draw-ings and paintings.

One thirteen year old, Noelani, felt stressed as her family prepared to return to the mission field for a second tour. The transition involved changing from a Christian school to a public one, moving to a different island in Hawaii, and being left in the care of another family while her parents raised support.

After Noelani read Barbara Johnson's book, *Splashes of Joy in the Cesspool of Life*, she applied one of its lessons to her situation. Noelani imagined herself in a huge white room with a stairway. At the top of the staircase, Jesus sat on a great white throne. Noelani had brought into the room a treasure chest which contained many things she loved. One by one, she took out her treasures, climbed the stairs, crawled onto Jesus' lap and explained to Him how much each thing or person meant to her. Then she handed the treasure to Him. The teenager didn't present all of the contents to Jesus at once because she wanted Him to know exactly what each one meant to her.

Noelani wept and gave Jesus her close friends at the Christian school she was leaving, her positions as a cheerleader and band member, and her involvement in school clubs. The process took over an hour, but in the morning Noelani felt more at peace that God loved her and was in control of her future. This helped her move ahead with the changes.

It's important to identify kids' individual bents or learning styles so we can help them develop prayer methods that will be lasting and meaningful to them. When we expect all children to approach God as we do, they can turn off to prayer. The Mover child may grow restless and fidgety with prolonged periods of quiet, staying-perfectly-still prayer and think that God is boring. But if we harness his energy in a prayer game, a prayer walk, or in making a box house (like a homeless person might live in) before praying for the street people in our city, he could consider prayer an adventure. The Talker child might get distracted if she has to pray silently in her room alone at bedtime, but she might really enjoy being part of a praying family or peer group. The Looker may need time and space alone to pray and write her conversations with God in a journal.

Keep in mind that spiritual gifting can impact children's prayer lives too. A girl with a gift of mercy may love praying with great compassion for hurting people. Another child might have a gift of evangelism and a burden to intercede for the nations. Young people with administrative gifts like to lead prayer and those with the gift of exhortation try to encourage *everyone* to pray. These gifts might also affect the "tools" kids use to pray. Some young pray-ers like a structured prayer calendar or list approach, while others flow with what the Holy Spirit is directing them to pray at a particular time.[1]

ROOM FOR INDIVIDUAL STYLE

With prayer, there is plenty of room for individual style. When we teach children to pray—or for that matter, when we pray—it's important not to confuse style with substance, or with spirituality. Based on prayers recorded in Scripture, God responds to stylistic variations from His pray-ers. The fact that we desire to communicate with Him matters more than *how* we talk to Him.

In the Bible people prayed various ways: with hands raised (Psalm 28:2), dropping to the knees (Luke 22:41), kneeling with eyes lifted to heaven (1 Kings 8:54), with clapping, dancing, and singing (Acts 16:25). There were shouted prayers (Joshua 6:16–20) and prayers without words (1 Samuel 1:12). The stylistic differences were both creative and indicative of each pray-er's personality, mood and requests.

Many joyful biblical prayers were sung to God (*see* Deuteronomy 32–33, Luke 1, and the Psalms). David spoke to the Lord in song on the day God delivered him out of the hands of Saul and his enemies. He sang, "The LORD is my rock, my fortress and my deliverer; my God is my rock, in whom I take refuge, my shield and the horn of my salvation" (2 Samuel 22:2–3).

When our children were young I often played my guitar as they sang favorite songs and Scripture choruses such as "We Bow Down" and "Wonderful Counselor." The children sometimes played rhythm instruments as we sang; they also made up their own songs. Now that our daughter is college-aged, she plays the guitar to God in praise, to pour out sadness or loneliness as well as joy. She best expresses her feelings to Him through music.

Recently I saw a mom and her two sons perform a worshipful dance to "The Little Drummer Boy." In their motions and dance, they interpreted the theme of "What can I give to you, Lord?" I have no doubt they delighted God's heart. Vicki, the mother, shared with me after their dance, "I've always related to David my whole life. David sang and danced in his prayers and he was a man after God's own heart. If that's how David acted, then I can follow that!" Her sons Colby and Conner, eleven and nine, started performing liturgical dance with her in their church several years ago. Both boys consider dance part of their prayer time at church and one of the best ways for them to feel God's presence.

When children move to praise music or dance, they can use flags, banners, or colorful strips of fabric or crepe paper to express their worship and prayer. They're happy to discover that movement can express joy and praise to God and that "sitting still" isn't the only way to pray!

"Signing" prayers is another effective way children can communicate with God through movement. My friend Penny took her kindergarten daughter, Abigail, to a class where they could learn the American sign language alphabet together. They learned to sign "The Lord's Prayer," "Away in a Manger," and other songs. Although Abigail is very young, she signs prayers and songs with her heart reverently focused on the Lord. When I saw fourteen children sign "Somebody's Praying for Me" at a Moms In Touch state retreat, it was a moving experience for the six hundred mothers present. The kids brought us into God's presence with their interpretation of the song through hand movements.

When we always pray in the same style, we can grow tired of praying. This is especially true for children, who love variety and hate ruts. "Get out of the ruts of prayer," advised W. H. P. Faunce, a classic theologian. "Pray sometimes standing up; then pray kneeling; then pray sitting down; then pray lying down on your couch at night."[2] What matters most is that we pray!

A CHANGE OF LOCATION

Just as we can vary our children's style of praying, we can also change the location in which they talk to God. In Scripture people uttered prayers on mountaintops (Exodus 19:23), in caves (1 Kings 19:9–10), and at sea (Jonah 2:1–9). People prayed in the sanctuary of the temple (Luke 1:8–10), on a rooftop (Acts 17:25), and in widows' houses (2 Kings 4:33). God's followers also prayed in difficult places like battlefields (Exodus 17:10–13), prison cells (Acts 17:25), a lion's den (Daniel 6:16–23), and a fiery hot furnace (Daniel 3:20–26).

There are so many different places we can pray, and our location preference is purely up to us. Some young people have a special prayer chair for their quiet times with God and like to light a candle nearby. One college student I know has a moving, prayer-on-the-go style that works for her busy days of juggling studies, job, and ministry. She praises God while fixing breakfast, confesses sin while showering, expresses thanksgiving while cycling to class, and petitions God all day as needs arise. Other kids pray best when they're in nature, walking on a trail or sitting by flowers.

We can convey to our children by our lifestyle that wherever we are, God is there too. He hears us whether we're in a classroom, in a beautiful national park surrounded by tall pine trees, or at the doctor's office. We can pray for neighbors while walking to the park, riding in the car, or doing household chores. We don't have to wait to pray about something until next week at Sunday school or until family devotions. We can pray any time, anywhere—and knowing this heightens kids' appreciation for God's greatness.

"Earth, with her thousand voices, praises God," wrote the poet Samuel Coleridge.[3] And in thousands of places, we can pray and praise Him.

MAKING THE CONTENT COUNT

But what about the content of kids' prayers? Do we teach them exactly what to say? Or ask them to repeat the same prayers over and over again? In some cases, as in a liturgy or the Lord's Prayer, recited prayers build security and stability. They connect us to the past and remind us of who we are as God's children. Prayer models, which we discussed earlier, also help kids learn to pray, giving them structure and motivation. But prayer is also as expansive as the God to whom we speak, able to encompass our kids' individuality. From free-wheeling shouts to whispered petitions to unintelligible groans, God hears and receives our prayers.

For example, my friend Louise's son, Jay, has Down's Syndrome and a deteriorating heart condition. Although Jay's retardation, speech disability, and health problems limit him in some ways, they have not inhibited the effectiveness of his prayers. When something happens, whatever the need is, Jay immediately prays about it. And though others might not understand his words, God does.

One day Jay's grandparents visited his home. Because of the ravages of Alzheimer's, his grandfather gets confused. The day they arrived Grandpa thought he'd lost his wife even though Grandma was standing beside him. He cried and grew so distraught that Louise had to drive them to a nearby hotel to calm him down and spend the night.

After breakfast the next day Louise retrieved her parents and brought them home. Sitting at the table, her father looked just as confused and upset as before. The adults did everything possible to make him comfortable, but he became more disoriented and sad. Suddenly Jay walked over to Grandpa, lay his hand on his shoulder and lifted the other hand to heaven. Then, simply, in his own garbled words, he asked God to heal Grandpa. The prayer ended with, "Thank You, God. Praise You, Jesus!" Within minutes Grandpa smiled, his mind cleared, and he knew who everyone was for the rest of the visit.

God's gracious acceptance of our prayers' content also means we can be honest with Him.

As a girl, I somehow thought God only liked hearing from me when I was cheerful and "doing everything right," that is, obeying my parents, reading the Bible, and being nice to friends. I thought He didn't want to hear about my sadness, anger, or worry. As I grew up I studied Scripture and discovered that God's people in the Bible prayed in many kinds of moods—when they were happy because they'd won battles, when they were frustrated over unanswered longings, when they sorrowed over someone's death. They cried out to the Lord when desperately afraid in a storm (Mark 4:35–38) or when grieved over the sinful condition of God's people, as Nehemiah did when he heard the walls of Jerusalem were broken down, the gates burned, and the people afflicted (Nehemiah 1:1–11). The prophet Habakkuk even railed against God, challenging Him to explain His ways with the nations. God not only listened, but answered.

Kids need to know they can be honest with God, that there isn't one "acceptable" mood or attitude for approaching Him. Yes, they need to confess sin and show reverence to the Lord. To nourish a thriving relationship with Him, they need to let go of bitterness and other barriers to heavenward communication. But loving God means giving all of ourselves to Him—expressing all the feelings He gave to us and all the difficulties that earth throws at us. Honesty and reverence aren't mutually exclusive.

David is a good role model of reverential honesty. In Psalm 120 he cries out to God in his trouble, even saying "Woe is me!" In many of the Psalms he pours out his heart and emotions, yet his focus is always God's mercy, greatness, and faithfulness. Studying the Psalms with an emphasis on how David balances honesty with reverence, giving God praise even in his lowest, darkest moments, can help young people feel free to pour out their own hearts to Him. Making "content count" in our prayers is opening our souls to the Creator.

FLEXING WITH OUR CHANGING KIDS

As a parent I've discovered that just when I think I've "figured out" my children, they hit another growth spurt and everything changes. What worked last month doesn't fly now; the devotional book they loved seems babyish to them. So for years I've kept a short prayer tacked on my bulletin board that says, "Lord, guide me through the transitions that are yet to come." It takes sensitivity to the Holy Spirit and our children, plus much flexibility, to adjust to the changing stages of their growing-up years.

As you try different prayer activities, you'll find that some will work better than others for your individual children's personalities and ages. What's important is to be open to variation instead of rotely saying the same words at the same time in the same way each day. By staying flexible, you'll instill excitement about how great God is and how creative He made us—so creative that we can enter His presence in many ways.

We can also be flexible to our kids' changing needs when we pray as a family. There may be some stages when a child is willing to pray aloud with the family, and other times when he prefers to pray silently. Older children may feel more freedom praying with friends at youth group instead of with Mom and Dad. As we approach them with love and acceptance in whatever stage they're in, we can ask, "Would you like to pray with me about this?" If they share a problem, that's great. But if we learn to not feel hurt or angry if the response is, "Not right now," then the prayer lines between us and our kids can stay open.

Even if we prayed with our teens every night as children, as adolescents they may want privacy at bedtime. Fern Nichols, founder of Moms In Touch International, says that when her daughter Trisha reached that stage she asked, "Trisha, could I just come in and pray a quick blessing over you before bed?" Trisha didn't mind that, so Fern said this blessing:

> O Heavenly Father, bless Trisha with the assurance that because she's Your child, You have declared her perfect in Your eyes, that You always care for her in her distresses of life. Father, bless her with the spiritual insight of knowing that You have set her apart for Yourself and Your will. Bless her with trust and hope in You. May the light of Your face shine down upon my Trisha.

We can give our children a blessing at bedtime, in the morning before school, and at special times like birthdays and graduations. We can speak our blessing, write it on a card or note, or even have it typeset and framed for their wall. Whatever our children's "bent" is or whatever stage they are in, a blessing assures them of our love and God's care.

We can model honesty and a lifestyle of loving communication with our heavenly Father. We can give our kids room and grace to be who God created them to be and encourage them to try different styles of prayer. We can be flexible as they pass through stages of growth and develop their own relationship with Him. But from there, we must relinquish control and trust the Holy Spirit to do His remarkable work. I find that the less I try to force change or be my kids' personal Holy Spirit, the more I pray and let God do His part, the more we all grow.

A Prayer of Thanksgiving

Thank You, Lord, that You created each of my children unique
and You desire fellowship with them.

Show them how to connect with You and abide in You.

Give them a heart that pursues You and a deep desire to pray.

Thank You for Your promise that when they seek You

with all their hearts,

they will find You.

May Your Spirit work within them

to give them a heart that cries, "Abba! Father!"

and to accomplish Your plans and purposes.

In Jesus' name, Amen.

HELPING KIDS PRAY

There are countless ways to help kids express their personal style in prayer.

- *Sports-fanatic kids* can pray for strength and good sportsmanship. They can thank God after a "win" or for something good that happened, but even after a loss, they can thank Him for the chance to compete.

- *Musical children* can sing their prayers. They can write original song-prayers or set any of the biblical psalms to a new melody and sing them to God.

    Playing "Musical Prayers" is a fun group activity. Like the game "Musical Chairs," children march around the chairs to the music and when it stops, quickly sit in the nearest chair. On each chair, write a prayer target such as, "Pray for the salvation of anyone at church today who doesn't know Jesus." Or, "Pray for the youth mission trip to Mexico." Then, for a short time, each child prays for the specific request taped to the chair before the music continues.

- *Visual children* can express prayers through drawings. Suggest that they draw someone who needs God's help or something they want to tell God. After family prayer, encourage them to draw what God is speaking to them about.

- *Verbal kids* love praying Korean-style. Korean people all pray aloud at the same time, which can be helpful to children who are adjusting to group prayer. Because everyone is talking, they don't feel on the spot or self-conscious.

- *Mover kids,* even those with short attention spans, can rejoice in spontaneous prayers and thanksgivings, sentence prayers aloud in the car and short, "popcorn prayers" aimed toward heaven.

    Out of a group of thirty or forty kids in children's church, there are always a number of "mover" children. One activity that has worked well for them involves tossing a large beach ball with a world map imprinted on it. After gathering the children in a circle, start some praise music and throw the ball from child to child.

When the music stops, whoever holds the ball puts his hand on a country and prays for the people to come to know Christ, for missionaries to be sent there, for churches to be planted, for Bibles to be available in their language, or for the children of that country.

To vary this method, place a giant map on the floor (of your city, state, nation, or world) and guide the children as they walk on it in synch to the music's beat. When the music stops, each child puts a hand on a specific place and prays for it.

- *Idea-oriented kids* may communicate with God more effectively by writing their prayers in a journal. Ten-year-old Krista started her own prayer journal this year, but with an organized twist to it. She assigned certain days of the week to specific prayer requests. Monday she prays for her friends at school. Tuesday, for two missionary families her family supports. Wednesday, for her sister and parents (her dad, a quadriplegic, needs special prayer and her mom is a children's minister at their church), and so-on through the week.

  Instead of tackling a long prayer list that overwhelms her, each day presents a different and manageable focus. Krista decorates her prayer journal with photos of the people for whom she's interceding, and saves room for the answers as she hears them. By recording these prayers and their answers, Krista is building a history with God, and growing more and more aware of His faithfulness.

- *Artistic types* enjoy creating devices to help them pray. Make a prayer chain by cutting out seven strips of construction paper in seven different colors. With markers, write on each strip who to pray for every day of the week:

Monday (Yellow)	*Mom, Dad, and grandparents*
Tuesday (Red)	*Sisters and brothers*
Wednesday (Orange)	*Friends at school*
Thursday (Blue)	*Missionaries*
Friday (Green)	*Senators and congressmen or*
	President and Vice-President
Saturday (Purple)	*Pastors*
Sunday (White)	*Church leaders and Sunday school teachers*

After making the individual links and decorating them with stickers and drawings, each child can tape them together into a prayer chain. At home the chain serves as a visual reminder to pray each day.

PART THREE

The Power of Group Prayer

We can pray every day

No matter where we are.

With friends or alone, even at home,

Our words must come from our heart.

MARY RICE HOPKINS
"Talk to You" from
Come Meet Jesus
Used by permission.

Dear God,
Thank you for my new baby brother! Please take care of Daddy on his trip.
Love, Chelsea

—*Chelsea, 8*

thank you for your unconditional love for me. thank you for always being there for me. even when that meant you had to die. i want to serve you jesus. i lay down all my hopes, dreams, and desires. show me how i can please you!

—*Hilary, 17*

Dear Heavenly Father,
Thank you for sending your only son down to earth to die on the cross for our sins so we can be saved and know you. And thank you for saving Jesus and letting him live forever. Amen

—*Brandon, 7*

CHAPTER TWELVE

The Family That Prays Together

*It is impossible to overstate the need for prayer
in the fabric of family life.*

JAMES DOBSON

C hildhood's learning is made up of moments. It isn't steady.
It's a pulse," wrote novelist Eudora Welty.[1]

"Prayer moments" are like that too. We can seize the big and small opportunities to gather our family together in prayer. Most daily hassles are great opportunities for the whole family to pray. Yet being "a family who prays together" doesn't require that we always sit around a table and work through a well-worn list. Nor does it mean we meet at the same time each day or week.

Please don't misunderstand. Regular, structured family prayer times are beneficial and meaningful, but as needs arise we can add or substitute "prayer moments" to a family's group prayer life as we allow both the planned and unexpected events to call our family to prayer.

Gail, a mother of four, told me, "When our family prayers became a struggle and our pre-teen was no longer interested, rather than fight it, we let prayer fall through the cracks. I wish we'd had some creative ideas to draw the kids into family prayer." Still, it's not too late for Gail to create prayer moments that pull a family together, and she can look into the "cracks" of life to do it.

ANYTHING AS A PRAYER REQUEST

When we look for prayer moments, anything and anyone in the family can initiate a prayer request that shoots through the family. We don't always have to be physically gathered together to "group pray" about a need.

Stephanie's five-year-old son Greg was terrified by the thought of starting kindergarten, even though the building was right across the street from their house. Greg had a hard time with any kind of change and loved staying home with Mom. In the months preceding the start of school, his anxiety increased with every mention of kindergarten, until finally they couldn't mention the "K" word in their house without Greg becoming hysterical.

At her wit's end, Stephanie held Greg in her arms and rocked him while she suggested asking for God's help.

"Do you believe God can help you?" she asked Greg.

"Yes, Mom, can we ask Him?"

"Dear God," Stephanie prayed, "Greg is five now and going through changes. He's going to start school soon and is very afraid. Please let Greg's angel put his hand on Greg's shoulder as he walks into school and let Greg know he's there. Give him strength and let something happen that will make him feel better about school. In Jesus' name, Amen."

Resting in his mom's arms, Greg didn't realize her request represented the prayers of a family. When Greg's dad, Carl, learned about his son's fears, he began praying too. Then he started praying individually with his son, and at other times, the whole family—Mom, Dad, Greg, and his two-year-old sister, Audrey—prayed together for him.

Day after day, these prayers calmed Greg and his mom until finally the first day of school came. With backpack in hand, Greg silently, reluctantly, and tearfully got dressed. Mom took his photo. They held hands and walked across the street to the school, talking about his angel.

Upon arrival to class, most of the kids said goodbye to their parents but Greg and another child cried.

"Why don't you walk around the halls to let Greg get familiar with the school?" the teacher suggested.

Mother and son walked to the water fountain, took a drink, and looked out at the playground.

Suddenly a voice called, "Greg!"

They turned and were surprised to see "Miss Lisa," his favorite swimming instructor from the local YMCA. Relief rushed over Greg's face. Someone he knew and loved! Her warm smile calmed him immediately, as Miss Lisa explained that she worked at the school.

After their chat and a hug from his friend, Greg walked confidently to class, hugged and kissed his mom and said, "Bye! See ya later!"

"Mom," said Greg later that night, "God sent Miss Lisa to be my angel, didn't He? He knew just what I needed!" Seeing how God took care of his fears, he began praying about everything. Now at the "grown-up" age of seven and a half, Greg regularly asks his parents to join him in praying for his younger sister who has spina bifida.

Lots of kids fear the dark, imaginary boogie men in their closets, lightning, and thunderstorms. They develop big worries over small things, and care about what seems inconsequential to us. We can brush away their concerns as childish or treat them as important opportunities for a family to pray. When we pray as a family about our children's fears and woes, wants and weaknesses, we teach them that everything about them matters to their family, that nothing is too small or impossible for God to do.

When we take our kids' concerns seriously, they'll learn to seriously follow God. Just like with Greg and his first day of kindergarten, our kids' problems can be the handle that helps a family draw closer to God.

GOD, OUR PROVIDER

"God, could you give me four more bugs?" Daniel prayed.

For weeks Daniel had searched for insects. He had carefully collected, identified, and mounted twenty-one bugs, but *twenty-five* was the teacher's requirement for a good grade. Time was running out and Daniel was fresh out of places to look for bugs. His mom thought this was a perfect opportunity for Daniel to see God work in his life. So Cynthia suggested her son pray for bugs.

Earnestly, Daniel offered his "four more bugs" prayer up to God at breakfast. When they went out to the garage a short time later to leave for school, there it was—a perfect mosquito—dead but intact, and right on the concrete! Then, as Daniel walked back into the house to put the mosquito in a safe place, jackpot! There lay a huge brown bug with fluorescent green markings, unlike anything he'd seen before. Daniel and his mom thanked God on the spot.

From bugs to school supplies, from urgently needed groceries to employment for parents, praying about practical stuff is right up a child's alley. Children love to pray for concrete items that visibly prove God answers prayer. Often parents think that praying for finances and other provisions is "adult work," and they don't want to "worry the kids," but when a family trusts God together for practical needs, children (and their parents!) experience His faithfulness first-hand.

The Thorpes, an Illinois family, desperately needed beds for their three children. Having outgrown their small beds, the kids were sleeping on the floor. But since the parents were committed to getting out of debt, charging the beds on a credit card was out of the question. "Our children prayed with us that God would provide beds, or open a way for us to find a good deal on used beds at a garage sale," says Meme, the mother. "We didn't know how He would provide, but the kids kept praying."

One night she and Rich, her husband, went out on a date. While the children were at home, a furniture store delivery truck pulled up and unloaded three brand-new beds.

"Who are these beds from?" they asked.

"We can't tell you; it's anonymous," the delivery man replied.

When their parents returned, the children questioned them. "Did you guys just go out and buy these beds for us? Who are these from?"

Just as surprised as their kids, Meme and Rich could only reply that the beds must be from God, because they didn't know anything about them.

The family dropped to their knees in the living room and thanked God together. Instead of watching their parents go into more debt, their children witnessed God's provision. They never did find out who sent those beds.

Sometimes, in our desire to fulfill all our kids' needs, we overextend our budget or go into debt instead of seeking God. How much better to let God supply, in His own time, and strengthen the faith of the entire family.

A FAMILY PRAYER PROJECT

Sometimes a loss or someone else's need creates not only a prayer moment, but a "prayer project" for your family. After Sally and her family moved to Florida, one of their closest friends, the father of six children, back home died suddenly. Sally, Don, and their children were saddened by the loss and frustrated by the hundreds of miles between their families. They wanted to attend the funeral, but couldn't. They wanted so much to do something practical to help, but couldn't.

Don wisely decided that the only thing they could do was actually the *best* thing they could do—pray. Together, the family committed to rise early every day for a week to pray for funeral arrangements, financial needs, comfort for the widow and her kids, and salvation for unbelievers attending the funeral. As the week progressed, they sensed that through their sacrificial prayers (they were sacrificing much sleep!), God not only brought help to the grieving family, but also comfort to the pray-ers themselves. Their sorrow turned to joy as they heard about specific ways God comforted and provided for their friends.

BUILDING A PRAYER HERITAGE

Praying together not only helps provide for a family's immediate needs, it also builds a spiritual heritage for its members.

Eight-year-old Eric lifted the glass jar from the kitchen's top shelf, brought it to the table, and poured out its contents. Flat river stones toppled out and the other siblings' hands rushed in to find their own special stones. Each rock was dated and had a few key words that reminded them of an event where they saw God at work in their family.

One rock thanked God for His protective power: *July 4, 1989. God uses Ryan to save Adam from drowning.* Other rocks commemorated God's faithfulness in small things, in a time of job layoff, and in the kids' school activities. *September 1989. God helps me not to be afraid of giving presentations in front of groups.*

The rock jar materialized when the children's father, Paul, was trying to find a way to explain the meaning of "Here I raise my ebenezer" from the hymn they sang in church. When he looked up the words in Joshua 4, he found that it referred to the twelve smooth river stones that Joshua constructed into a memorial. As Joshua and the elders finished the "monument" of stones, he said, "In the future, when your children ask you, 'What do these stones mean?' tell them that the flow of the Jordan was cut off before the ark of the covenant of the LORD.... These stones are to be a memorial to the people of Israel forever" (Joshua 4:6–7).

Just as the Israelites' stones served as a concrete reminder of God's intervention on their behalf, so Paul and his children gathered rocks to make their own remembrance. When they take out the jar to add new stones or look at old ones, they retell the stories of God's provision and rekindle their sense of awe and gratitude toward God.[2]

Whether you have a prayer journal that records God's acts, a scrapbook, or, like the Moede family, a collection of stones, find a way to remember what God has done for your family through answered prayer. You'll be creating a history of your walk with God as well as a wonderful legacy of faith for your children.

When Colby Robinson left a parochial school and entered public school, he asked his mom, "Do they have chapel every morning like our other school?" When he found out they didn't, he said, "Then we need to have chapel here at home. Could we?"

That started the Robinson's morning chapel service with music as their call to worship. Mom sings a hymn or praise chorus while Dad and the three boys join in singing wherever they are in the house, on their way to the prayer corner. The corner is decorated with art, Bible verses, and Sunday school crafts for the changing seasons. On the table are candles, several versions of the Bible, and a children's devotional.

Here's where the family prays for guidance and wisdom—for Colby's dyslexia and God's help with his learning, or for the older son's need for self-control. They read Scripture together and pray about the day before leaving for school and work. But most of all, they build a prayer heritage, together as a family.

PASSING ALONG THE PRAYER

The marvelous thing about prayer is that it can be passed along, and as a family we can bless others with our intercession. Beyond establishing prayer projects, we can incorporate prayer into hospitality, caring about the people who pass through our home for an evening or an extended visit.

When our daughter prepared to leave Kansas City after an internship in youth ministry, the family of one of the teens she had worked with invited her for dinner. After a delicious meal, they asked, "Can we pray for you, Alison?"

Children and parents gathered around our daughter as she sat on the couch. Truman, the six year old, prayed first and the others joined in. "Lord, bless Alison in her new start in college."

"Light her path," said another child.

"Put Your arms around her and let her know You're with her, that You will always direct her steps."

"Provide friends for her, Lord."

Alison marveled at how sensitive the children were to God's Spirit and that they prayed for some of her biggest concerns.

Later I asked Becky, the mom, how she organized this warm way of blessing guests. She explained, "We all get together and I just say, 'Let's go in order, around the circle.' Since they all follow the sibling next to them, there are no big periods of silence. But there's no time limit. Sometimes Truman, the youngest, prays five or ten minutes."

When they first started inviting singles and college students over for dinner, the family felt God wanted them to bless their visitors by praying for them. Becky prepared her children with a few tips: "Pray whatever God puts in your heart for this person. Don't be afraid; say whatever comes to your mind." Of course, it helps to talk and get to know a person during the meal. But with the children, they often say and pray things that are right on target, even when it's someone they've only known for an evening!

As your family grows, I encourage you to harness the power of group prayers—for each other, for their world, and as blessings on those who visit your home.

A Prayer for Our Family

Lord, thank You for our family.

I want our home to be established on the rock of Your Word

and sustained by Your Spirit as we pray and trust You.

I pray for Your protection and care for our children

and for the wisdom to rear them tenderly

in the training and counsel of the Lord.
Let me be an imitator of You and copy Your example, Jesus,
as well-beloved children imitate their father.
In Your Name, Amen.

HELPING KIDS PRAY

How can your family get started if you haven't been praying regularly together? Here are some ideas to provide a beginning, or to refresh your prayer time if it has become rote:

- *A basket of blessings.* A small basket in the middle of the dinner table can be a springboard for family prayer. Fill the basket with Christmas photo cards and pictures of friends, grandparents, and missionaries. Each child picks out a photo at the meal and prays for that person.

  A family I know takes it a step further. They send out a red "Merry Christmas" postcard that says, "It is our family's tradition to take each Christmas card we receive and pray for the family sending it. We prayed for you on January 10th." They sign their names and include a special Scripture blessing.

- *Praying hands.* Physical things we can touch, like the memorial stones we saw in this chapter, provide a great contact point for prayer. Claire, a missions coordinator, travels to conferences occasionally. When she is gone overnight, she carries her daughter Devon's handprint with her. At a pre-arranged time, they both place their hands on the other's handprint and pray. Although in another city or in another state, Claire feels close to her daughter as she places her hand on the print and prays at the appointed time.

- *"The best part of the day."* Karen, a Kansas mom, brings a positive spin to her daughters' bedtime prayers, and gives each girl a chance to talk about herself and that day. Emphasizing the good sets the stage for praying with gratitude. Then they thank God for the "best part of the day" before lifting up prayer requests.

- *Good questions.* Encourage kids to talk to God by asking questions such as these:

  What was the happiest thing that happened today? Let's thank God for that.

  What was sad at school, or something you felt bad about or struggled with, that we could pray about?

  Was there something today you did that you need to ask Jesus' forgiveness for?

  If you could ask God to do anything in your life at this time, or help you with something, what would it be?

CHAPTER THIRTEEN

Small Groups, Big Answers

What might God do in a prayed-for world?
It's likely that God has never had such a thing before,
in which every breathing person has been prayed for
by caring Christians.
Step into this movement of holy expectancy.
God will not bring revival by surprise.
Scripture hints that God will be pleased to visit
a prayed-for world.

STEVE HAWTHORNE

One spring my husband Holmes and I accepted the responsibility of training young people to function in prayer teams, ready to minister to the congregation at the close of the annual Youth Service at our church.

Each team consisted of four teens who stood by the kneelers at the front of the sanctuary during ministry time. Then as congregation members each presented their requests on a slip of paper, the kids prayed conversationally, in one accord, for the grown-ups in their church—people who had been their Sunday school teachers, choir leaders, parents, and others. What a blessed time!

Through this event we learned that the words "in one accord" and "conversational" are crucial concepts for small group pray-ers. One-accord praying is "agreeing together as directed by the Holy Spirit." [1] This kind of group prayer is based on Jesus' promise in Matthew 18:19–20: "Again, I tell you that if two of you on earth agree about anything you ask for, it will be done for you by my Father in heaven. For where two or three come together in my name, there am I with them."

Have you ever participated in a prayer group in which requests were presented, then talked about for so long that there was little time left except for a brief, general prayer? Or perhaps the participants, after hearing five or ten requests, prayed about them shotgun style, hitting some and jumping to others? Or maybe one long-winded, well-intentioned person got carried away, praying a wearisome, thirty-minute prayer and the other participants didn't pray at all?

On the other hand, when a group of children or adults pray in agreement, the participants are actually asking the Holy Spirit to align them with God's will in a matter. To this end, the participants focus only on one subject at a time, praying conversationally rather than trying to impress God (or anyone else) with the "right words."[2] Practically speaking, here is how conversational, one-accord prayer works. The leader presents a prayer topic, collected from the group members, and someone prays a sentence about it. Then another person in the circle might pray a Scripture that relates to it, and the group sticks to that subject until it seems well covered in prayer. The group doesn't bounce around from Mary's sprained ankle to Jana's sick grandma to Jerry's school problem. More than one person can pray different aspects of the subject. When the topic has been thoroughly covered, the group senses this and pauses for a moment of silence. After that, the pray-ers can focus on a new topic.

For example, when the kids listed prayer requests in the kindergarten to third grade Sunday school class last winter, Jessica, a second grader, wanted prayer for her broken arm. A doctor had set the arm the day before, and it still ached. In response, the adult leaders suggested that the children circle around Jessica and pray about her need.

"Lord, help Jessica's bone heal quickly," prayed Marquise.

"Please take away her pain," said Joel.

"Give Jessica patience as her arm knits together," I prayed.

"Jesus, wrap Your arms around Jessica. Let her know she can come to You," added Polly. The group continued until Jessica and her broken arm were completely bathed in the love and concern of her classmates and she was comforted by God's Spirit.

With the teens who ministered on Youth Sunday, I suggested they stick to the person's need expressed on a slip of paper, to avoid dominating with long prayers. "Listen to the Holy Spirit. Pray short, from-your-heart prayers," I coached. "Don't feel it all depends on you to pray everything; trust that with all four of you listening to God, He'll speak to each team member about what to pray." The students caught on fast and led a wonderful ministry session.

In both situations the kids discovered that with group prayer, sincerity matters more than formality, and listening more than talking.

GROUP PRAYER GOES ANYWHERE

Small prayer groups for children and youth don't necessarily have to originate in a church or organization. They can form in homes, schools, neighborhoods—anywhere kids want to pray together about mutual and individual concerns. They can be structured or flexible and incorporate toddlers to teens. The important element is that they give kids a secure, consistent place to pray.

Two home school moms, Julie Brown (a missionary serving with AmeriTribes in Arizona) and her friend Linda, started a prayer group once a week to teach their kids prayer as a lifestyle. Julie and Linda didn't want their children to wait until they grew up to develop a small group prayer life or be involved in their church's mission to the world. So they created "Kids Pray." And with their eight energetic children, it's quite a group!

Since the children range from preschoolers to age thirteen, Julie and Linda divide up their "Kids Pray" time into four short segments of fifteen minutes each so the time passes quickly but productively. For the first fifteen minutes the mothers accommodate their children's "wiggles" through games, songs, and activities to help the kids praise God and prepare their young hearts for prayer. In the next fifteen minutes they pray for leaders—their dads, their pastor, and even the president of the United States. The next segment focuses on unreached peoples, and the last quarter hour is spent praying for missionaries.

Julie believes prayer is not just sitting quietly with hands folded in laps, eyes closed, and heads bowed. "Perhaps it is that mentality that hinders us (and particularly children) from continually offering up prayers," she says. Accordingly, when the kids prayed for missionary friends in Tatarstan, the children put their hands in a grab bag and pulled out photos of the family, airline tickets, medicine, and a report card. Each child then prayed for the need that a selected object represented (safety in travel, health, the kids' schooling, etc.).

These two moms also periodically bring food to the prayer group. As the children sample Chinese, Indian, Italian, Mexican, or Thai cuisine, they learn about another part of the world and pray for that country during its "fifteen minutes of fame." In addition to tickling the tastebuds, these meals have cultivated the children's interest in missions.

Hannah, age eight, has prayed for Malay Muslims ever since college students from that country visited her home. TJ, Julie's oldest son, prays for Pankwat, a boy his age in Nigeria. The two eleven-year-old boys write letters, exchange pictures, and pray for one another. TJ also tithes some of his money to help Pankwat buy and care for chickens to supplement his family's income. Pankwat, in turn, writes to TJ about how the money is providing medicine and food. As a result, TJ is interested in Africa and concerned for the well-being of persecuted believers in Nigeria.

Julie and Linda also help their kids keep prayer journals. The younger children record their prayers with drawings and photos, while the older kids write out their requests and decorate the pages with stickers. Periodically, the group reviews the journals and thanks God for answered prayer.[3] In the future, the journals will serve as "history books," first-hand and cherished records of God's faithfulness toward eight kids who discovered the joy of one-accord group prayer.

A GROUP PRAYER ADVENTURE

If an ongoing prayer group is too big a commitment for some kids, they can still experience one-accord intercession by attending events or tagging along on creative outings planned by prayer-conscious adults.

One Sunday I accompanied kids on a prayer walk around the city jail and police station. It was a sunny but cold, blustery Sunday morning as thirty-five children and several adults donned coats to pursue our "mission." Before leaving for our destination, though, we prepared with praise, confession, thanksgiving, and seeking God's will for our intercession. On a big white board I wrote what the kids thought God wanted for the inmates.

"He'd want them to know Jesus," said Ben.

"Freedom," said Joel. "They want to get out of jail!"

We talked about the "freedom within" that God desired for them—release from the bondage to drugs, alcohol, or other addictions that trapped the inmates in sin.

"That they'd know God's love," said a thoughtful Kendall.

"How can they know that love?" I asked.

They all agreed we needed to ask God to send people to share His love. And for the inmates to repent and accept God's forgiveness.

"Their kids!" piped up Morgan.

We agreed that praying for their children was important, because it would be very sad to have your dad or mom in jail.

Next, an adult assigned each of the seven small groups one of the prayer topics we'd highlighted: salvation, repentance, people to bring God's love (and for the guards to know Christ and be vessels of His love), freedom, protection, and the inmates' children. Then out we went, praying as we walked to the jail.

The group leaders started with prayer for their topics and whatever came to mind. Some kids prayed for the policemen as they passed their cars; others prayed for the lawyers and workers as they approached their offices next door to the jail. Some children prayed aloud and others prayed silently. And several just remarked that they felt cold!

After we had walked around the entire building, we formed a circle and Rob, one of the dads, led us in prayer and thanksgiving. We assured the kids that God would use their prayers to bring about His will for people in the jail. And who knows—they might meet someone in heaven someday who will say, "I'm here because you prayed for me that Sunday when I was in jail." God specializes in giving big answers to small groups of pray-ers.

As we gathered back in a warm upstairs, the children shared their thoughts. After a few minutes one of the younger children spoke. "In my mind I saw a policeman and he was trying to push his car over a man he was chasing. He was mean because he was angry at the bad man," she said. We took her story seriously and prayed for this policeman to have wisdom and compassion, and for him to know Christ.

Then eight-year-old John raised his hand and said, "This verse kept coming into my mind while we were walking around the jail: 'Let the little children come to me, and do not hinder them, for the kingdom of heaven belongs to such as these'" (Matthew 19:14).

We thanked God together that this is true: He's calling the children to come to Him, not only in our city that morning, but in prayer groups around the world.

A Prayer for Group Ministry

Thank You, Father, for the gift of prayer
and the privilege of praying
with our sisters and brothers in Christ.
Thank You that You promise a special effectiveness
when we pray with others in agreement.
Show me those children, young people, or adults
You want me to partner with in prayer.
Then lead our group by Your Spirit,
showing us what's on Your heart
so we can agree with You.
In Jesus' name, Amen.

HELPING KIDS PRAY

Want to gather up a group? Here are some tips on leading children in group prayer.

- *If you have a large number of children, divide into small groups.* The first time I helped lead children in prayer for a special missions outreach, we divided forty kids into groups of eight to ten. We quickly discovered the groups were too big. The quiet children didn't pray at all, and some kids got rowdy. Now the children pray in groups of four to six, and everyone gets involved and cooperates.

   Each group needs a leader to help the members stay focused on their prayer targets. The leader can be an adult, college student, high school or junior high student. He or she is a coach, not a dictator. The leader should avoid praying too long so kids won't tune out, and should try to involve shy children by asking, "Would you pray about this?"

- *Prepare for group time.* If it's a prayer walk, find people in the church who know about the geography, politics, and history of the area. Map out your path and strategy. Even if it's a very small group that meets to pray in your home, employ one of the prayer models from chapter 6 to create a flexible structure before the kids arrive. Otherwise, the session might meander, they'll lose interest, and you'll be frustrated.

- *Help kids form friendships.* Whether young or old, when people pray together, the Lord knits them together in friendship. To facilitate this caring, you might consider offering a time during the group meeting when kids are paired together to pray for each other's greatest need that day or week. Also, before or after the group prayer, allow time for fellowship.
- *Wait on God.* Don't be afraid of silence at the beginning of your prayer gathering or at any point in the process of intercession. When you gather kids to pray, encourage them to ask God what is on His heart, then wait for Him to speak through Scripture, visual pictures, or His still, small voice. Being sensitive to God's Spirit can bring forth powerful prayer.
- *Provide variety.* It's easy for a prayer group to get in a rut of doing the same thing every week. That's why it's important to listen to God's Spirit for His guidance. When He leads us, no matter how many years we pray, it continues to be an adventure!

Joyce Satter says, "Worship, intercession, and prayer are creative, spontaneous encounters with God" that can't be put into a box or fixed-in-concrete curriculum.[4] Our creative God is full of surprises, and as we follow Him and stay tuned to His Spirit, there is joy and adventure when we meet with others to pray.

lord
i pray that i will have a desire every day to know you more.
you can show me new things every day, especially when i'm
having my quiet time and worshiping. you you are the best
thing that ever happened in my life. i love you so much. love
your daughter. betsy

—Betsy, 14

Dear God,
Thank you for dieing on the cross. Thank you for my family and friends and
my church. Thank you for children's church. Love, Stephen

—Stephen, 9

dear heavenly father.
please be with my friends in public schools. help them to be
salt and light for you amen.

—Emily, 15

CHAPTER FOURTEEN

Praying Kids on Campus

Let no one look down on your youthfulness...
Show yourself an example of those who believe.

THE APOSTLE PAUL

As a high school freshman Stacy Hanson attended her youth group's "Snow Camp" winter retreat. One night she sang with the other kids, "If You can use anything, You can use me." Suddenly she broke down crying and prayed, "God, You can have everything, all of me, all my hopes and dreams."

Stacy sensed that God replied, "If you give everything to Me, I can do wonders through you." As she prayed later, she felt God challenging her to reach twenty friends for Christ before the end of her sophomore year.

"Twenty, Lord?" It sounded like a huge task.

Returning to her home in Minneapolis, this teen began rising an hour earlier to pray for classmates. The youth group had set up a prayer chain for the school year, and Stacy's link was at 6 A.M. Day after day she prayed for Blaine High School students during that hour.

Months later Stacy learned that the play, "Heaven's Gates, Hell's Flames," would be performed at her church, and she decided to invite a few of the friends on her prayer list. The "few" friends grew to many.

"I spent the weekend before calling fifty school friends and inviting them to the play," says Stacy. About fifteen agreed to attend the first performance. "They were my closest friends, none with Christian backgrounds. I was excited," she adds. That night, at the end of the performance, a cast member gave an invitation. All fifteen classmates accepted Christ as their Savior.

There were two more evening performances, so Stacy invited more friends. The next night she took ten teens to the play, and all accepted Christ.

With one night left, God nudged Stacy to invite the "popular kids"—the cheerleaders and football players and even some of the drug and party crowd.

"Oh, Lord, what if they make fun of this? What if they think it's too spiritual?" Stacy felt scared, but obeyed God and invited them anyway. Twenty students accompanied Stacy to the play. At the end of the performance, the captain of the football team stood up and the other kids followed him down the aisle to receive Christ.

Over a few days, *forty-five* teens had accepted salvation.

"God used my tiny little mustard seed of faith to work a miracle in my friends' lives," Stacy says. In the following weeks these kids contacted Stacy every day, asking her questions about the Bible and how to walk with God. This challenged her faith again, and she found other mature Christian students to help answer their questions.

A few days after these teenagers became Christians, Stacy planned on participating in "See You at the Pole," the annual event in which students meet around the flagpole and pray for their school. She decorated invitations with flag stickers and put them in the lockers of the forty-five new Christians, asking them to join her in prayer. These new believers had never attended a prayer gathering, yet forty-three showed up, one-third of the total number of kids gathered around the flagpole that morning.

Many of the "regular crew" of Christian kids were surprised. "What are you doing here?" one of them asked a guy who, prior to the play, had only used God's name as a cuss word.

"I accepted God and we're praying for the school!" he answered. He joined a former drug user, the head cheerleader, football players— a total of 130 kids—who asked God to draw their friends to Christ. Stacy wept for joy the entire day.

THE GROWING YOUTH PRAYER MOVEMENT

All across America young people like Stacy want to make a difference for Christ on campus. One evidence is the tremendous growth of youth prayer gatherings like See You at the Pole (SYATP). Last fall I stood with more than 125 students at Douglas County High School in Castle Rock, Colorado. In the center of the group, a flagpole anchored the American flag against a brisk morning wind.

For a few minutes the teens held hands and sang. As the singing ebbed, a red-headed girl in a gray sweatshirt prayed aloud, "Lord, I want my classmates to know You. Thank You for all these kids who came. It gives me courage to know I'm not the only Christian on campus."

"I praise you for giving us your Son so we can live with You forever," a boy prayed. Kids shivered in the cold air as they interceded for classmates who were troubled, confused, or didn't know Christ.

"Fill us with compassion for our friends. Help us reach them."

"Let them see You through us. Let us be lights."

"Make us sensitive to Your Spirit and to be bold in You, God."

Traffic raced on the nearby highway and curious students filed by, but the "pole kids" stayed focused. They knew that around the world on that day more than three million elementary, junior high, senior high, and college students were praying around flagpoles too.

A SMALL BEGINNING

See You at the Pole is a huge prayer movement now, but it began small, when a group of Texas teens drove to schools in the dark of night and prayed. Broken before God and burdened for their classmates, they asked God for a spiritual awakening. They didn't know their obedience would eventually beckon millions of young people to pray for their campuses—as far away as Moscow and the Ivory Coast of West Africa. They only wanted to pray for their friends.

The year 1990 was significant for the youth at Crestmont Baptist Church in Burleson, Texas. Rick Eubanks, music and youth minister, wanted the teenagers to be "missionaries" on campus. Through praise and worship, discipleship and teaching, he prompted their prayer lives to deepen. The kids changed from singing songs *about* Jesus to singing *to* Jesus and entering His presence. And they had a growing desire for their high schools to turn to Christ.

One Friday night on a "discipleship weekend," youth pastor Kyle Kelly encouraged a small group of kids to be more involved in reaching their campuses. After the session the teenagers felt God wanted them to pray on-site at their schools. So around midnight, they visited the grounds of two junior high schools and one house where a student was home schooled. They claimed the campuses for Christ, praying for individual students. It was a powerful weekend of prayer. From there, one of the students started a campus group called "GAP," for "God and Prayer." He made T-shirts and invited other students to commit to pray for the school.

As students prayed for their classmates, a movement began to grow. Brian, one of the most popular teens in Burleson High School, had been saved in the sixth grade but had fallen away from God. He belonged to the youth group but had also become the leader of the wrong crowd at school.

"We knew he had such potential, and we prayed constantly for him," said Rick. He prayed, "God, get him out of the relationships he's in. Wake him up. Do what's necessary to get Brian back—turn the heat up on this guy!" For over a year the youth leader and the kids prayed for Brian.

One day Brian called Rick to talk about a relationship gone bad and other pressures. "I know I'm going the wrong direction," the teen admitted. Brian recommitted his life to Jesus Christ. But he didn't stop there. He contacted his friends and said, "Hey! We're going in the wrong direction!" He prayed for twenty-three guys, got them together for Bible studies and led all of them to Christ. These young men took other new Christians under their wings and the spiritual influence on campus multiplied.

These events inspired another pastor, Chuck Flowers, to corral students around their schools' flagpoles for prayer, and See You at the Pole was born. Rick, Chuck, and other youth pastors thought perhaps 20,000 students would participate that year, but news about the event trickled to other churches via students who had attended the Super Summer School, a discipleship school on a Texas campus.

Word had spread. Forty-five thousand kids showed up at their flag-poles for the first See You at the Pole event on the third Wednesday of September, 1991. Rick and Chuck rejoiced, but considered it only a one-time, statewide event. But the wind of God's Spirit moves where it will, and the prayer event spread. In some schools a student stood alone at the pole. But soon others followed and the number of praying young people grew, not just on SYATP Wednesday, but throughout the school year. In the years since that initial meeting, thousands of student-led Bible clubs and regular prayer meetings have formed.

STANDING ALONE

Tom Andes, an Ohio high school student, was one of those who prayed alone at the flagpole for his campus. During a senior high youth retreat, Tom's youth pastor had challenged him to take a stand for God, and Tom had responded by promising the 300 attendees that he would pray for his school every day. His youth pastor was grateful for Tom's new enthusiasm, but quietly wondered if he could keep his commitment.

In blazing sunshine and on icy cold mornings, Tom prayed at the flagpole of his high school—alone. He prayed for the teachers, the principal, the other students, and the leaders of our country. He prayed for kids addicted to drugs, for those causing violence at his school, for the salvation of every person on the campus.

Tom prayed by himself for a month, but then another student joined him. On some days, Tom's youth pastor joined them. By Christmastime, ten students prayed with Tom every day. In another three months twenty-four students committed to daily intercession for their campus. By that summer the idea had spread to seven of the nine high schools in that Ohio county and four high schools in the next county.

"Because one young person was faithful to God, 150 kids in Northeast Ohio started to pray every day," explains Stan Heeren, Tom's youth pastor.[1]

Nobody knows when SYATP will end or how God will use the students' prayers in the future, but this campus movement is still growing. In 1997 teens in Russia met at Lenin's tomb; others gathered at the Kremlin to pray. Kids in Guam, Japan, South Korea, and Turkey prayed for their campuses. Students of all grades, skin colors and denominations have prayed around flagpoles on military base high schools, in European countries, and throughout America. God continues to move at their high schools and bless the pray-ers' lives.

TILLING THE GROUND

God is also raising up intercessors on college campuses, even using some "unlikely" prayer warriors. When Jeremy, a University of Tennessee student, entered college, he lived in a fog of drugs, alcohol, and fraternity house smoke during his freshman and sophomore years. But a serious car crash after a party broke bones, severed his radial nerve, and paralyzed his right arm. The accident turned him to God.

After months of recovery at home, Jeremy returned to the campus with his spiritual eyes open. "It was familiar territory but different because I saw it through changed eyes," he remembers.

God gave Jeremy a tremendous burden for the campus and its students, but at first the young man was overwhelmed by a sense of heaviness and depression. There was so much darkness on campus that it felt too big for him to handle by himself. Eventually, Jeremy realized that God had sent him back as a missionary, and connected him with David, another Christian student. On two different days they walked around the university and prayed, focusing their intercession on whatever the Spirit directed them to say.

In his mind's eye, Jeremy felt that the main demonic principality at the university was located on top of the Humanities and Social Sciences building, the hub of the campus. From there, the tentacles of humanism and vain philosophies spread out to every building and department of the university.

Like Joshua and Caleb shouting down the walls of Jericho, the boys took authority over addictions and alcohol abuse. They repented for the sins of the student body. They asked God to shut down the fraternity and sorority houses and turn them into places of prayer. They walked "The Strip," a street lined with bars where students went to get drunk, praying and claiming the area for Christ.

All this time God showed Jeremy marvelous things—there would be praise bands on Friday and Saturday nights; the frat and sorority houses would someday be sources of revival. They prayed around the huge football stadium (the biggest one in America, seating 107,000) and believed God planned to make it a place of prayer, praise rallies, and student-led revival meetings.

When the two boys walked to classes every day for that year, they continued to pray for the students, for God to remove ungodly professors and administrators and for salvation for every student and staff member. Jeremy says, "We pray everywhere we go. I ask God to show me who I can tell about Him, and for the Holy Spirit to go before me and fill me with His love."

Jeremy is a senior now, ready to graduate, but he believes their prayers laid spiritual groundwork at the University of Tennessee. He's confident that other prayer warriors will claim the campus and, in God's timing, the Holy Spirit will move on this campus. Like the first wave of troops sent in by the military, God sent two prayer warriors before the invasion!

PRAYER STORM

Young people are not only praying for their campuses, but for revival in our nation. Since 1996 several thousand young people have prayed every week for a spiritual awakening in America as part of Rock the Nation's "Prayer Storm."

Students from around the country commit to prayer and fasting one day a week, with specific prayer targets. They're praying for God to bring revival to their lives, families, friends, and school. They're crying out to God for renewal in their churches, in the nation, and throughout the world. In Prayer Storm events in various cities, students meet to "storm heaven" together for spiritual revival in America.

The Prayer Storm movement grew out of God's direction to Rusty Carlson during a forty-day fast by the Rock the Nations staff in 1996. He felt God was calling the students of America to prayer, fasting, and repentance on behalf of the country and their generation. At the next Rock the Nations event, half of the students committed to weekly prayer and fasting.

As the numbers continue to grow, Rusty envisions a generation of kids significantly different from the secular media's depiction of them as an aimless subculture plagued by drugs and out-of-wedlock pregnancies. Rusty believes God has a bigger plan for "Generation X" and the younger "Millennium Generation." He knows that many aggressively pursue God, and that students are getting on their knees with a desire to impact their world for Christ.

ABOUT YOUTH-LED REVIVAL

What will happen as young people like Jeremy, Tom, Stacy, and the others continue to storm heaven, if thousands of youth keep praying around flagpoles for their schools, teachers, and communities? If past generations give any indication, we may be on the threshold of a great awakening, a true revival.

> In all ages the great creative religious ideas have been the achievement of the intellectual and spiritual insight of young men...evidenced by such names as Jesus, St. Francis of Assisi, Loyola, Huss, Luther, Erasmus, Wesley, and Mott.... Many of the most revolutionary ideas have been worked out by young men under thirty and frequently by youths between eighteen and twenty-five.[2]

In the 1790s and 1890s students led America in spiritual awakenings and renewals. The Welsh Revival at the turn of the century was led by twenty-one-year-old Evan Roberts; many of his ministry helpers were in their late teens. In the 1950s, newspapers carried stories of the college revival sweeping campuses, which started a missions movement unparalleled in its impact. A campus revival broke out during chapel services at Asbury College in Kentucky in 1970 and spread to more than 130 colleges and seminaries. In 1995, prayer and God's Spirit brought revival to Wheaton College, from which revival spread to many other campuses and churches.[3]

Today, earnest prayer on campuses is stirring up revival again. Although many teens of this generation are still caught in self-destructive behavior, God is moving mightily among our youth. The world's greatest revival and harvest of souls could begin with them. That's the kind of miracle God loves to supply when children pray.

A Prayer for Youth

Heavenly Father, as I continue to plant seeds in my children's lives
and water them with prayer, I pray for a great harvest—
that my children will grow to be young people You can use mightily
to lead many others to Christ,
to impact their high school and college campuses,
and even the world.
Grant devotion to You and wisdom beyond their years
to this generation of youth, and use them for Your glory!
In Jesus' name, Amen.

HELPING KIDS PRAY

No matter how pumped you are about See You at the Pole, Prayer Storm, or other youth prayer events, pushing your teen to participate probably won't work. Let me offer suggestions for encouraging teens to participate on their own.

- *Ask questions, but let your teen make the decision.* You could ask if your child has heard of SYATP (or another prayer event), and describe it, perhaps telling him where he can get more information if he's interested. But let your teen decide whether to participate. Attending because Mom or Dad said "you have to" is not the best motive.

- *Pray for your teenagers and let the Holy Spirit guide them.* The Holy Spirit is drawing young people to Himself and giving them a heart for prayer. But we need to remember that each of our kids is different, and some are more drawn to prayer than others. We need to be sure we're not acting as our teens' "Personal Holy Spirit," or manipulating them to do something that's not in their hearts. If we do, we could hinder God's work in them.

    Proverbs 3:5–6 applies to parents. It advises us to trust in God with all our hearts instead of leaning on our own understanding, our own control. Pray with all your might for the Holy Spirit to draw your child, and for relationships to develop with other Christian teens who stand for Christ and pray for their campuses. Pray for their youth leaders and pastors. And pray for patience!

    Lee Brown, a praying mother who has seen revival in her kids' Tennessee high school, says, "If you want to see your children live for Christ and your school and community change, be committed to persistent prayer. Prayer is one of our major weapons of warfare because the enemy is coming full force against our children and schools. We've got to use the weapon God has given us!"[4]

- *Encourage them to be involved with the youth group* at your church, where they'll hear about upcoming youth events and gatherings. Attending a SYATP event or campus outreach with friends eases apprehensions. Belonging to a vibrant youth group is a tremendous support to their growing faith. They can learn to pray in fellowship with others their age and be discipled in Bible, prayer, and evangelism.

CHAPTER FIFTEEN

Prayers Heard 'Round the World

Heaven is calling! Jesus is waiting!
He is waiting for teenagers, women, children, and men
to embrace the high call of priestly intercession.

ALICE SMITH

The morning air danced with excitement as delegates from the Seventh Congress of the National Children's Prayer Network walked the few short blocks from their hotel to the White House's Old Executive Office Building.

It was the National Day of Prayer, May 1, 1997. Radio and television stations were covering the events as hundreds of Christians filled the city to intercede for the country, listen to speakers, and attend prayer rallies. However, few heard about the enthusiastic young prayer warriors from different schools and cities who also had gathered there to pray.

Late the night before, 150 delegates found out they would meet with the vice president at exactly 11 A.M. the next day. The children considered this a great honor. They had spent many hours in prayer during their stay in Washington, D.C., praying with legislators, ambassadors, and other important leaders in the city. This meeting would culminate this important week of prayer and ministry.

When Vice President Al Gore entered the room, the protocol began. Introductions ensued, and two of the children prayed for him and his family. Mr. Gore thanked the children and shared how prayer had impacted his life and family.

The vice president talked about the difficult ordeal his family had faced in 1987 when his young son Albert was hit by a car on the way to a baseball game. Mr. Gore remembered that while Albert lay in the hospital with critical injuries, a pre-kindergarten class began to pray for him. Mrs. Story had brought a newspaper article into the classroom and encouraged the children to pray for Albert. The children along with their teacher took on the prayer request with faith and enthusiasm. Later they wrote cards and letters of encouragement to the Gore family. Now, ten years later, another group of children had come to pray for him.

After finishing the story about how God's healing grace had brought about his son's recovery, Mr. Gore challenged the children to continue to pray daily. He reminded them that prayer not only changes things, but it also changes us.[1]

A NATIONAL CHILDREN'S NETWORK

The children at the National Prayer Congress represented children from Christian school classrooms and churches in America who belong to the National Children's Prayer Network. These children take seriously the duty to pray for national leaders.

"Envision raising a generation of leaders who know how to reach heaven through intercession," says Lin Story, the network's founder. Her goal is to challenge youth of all ages to recognize their potential in prayer, to train them in the principles of intercession, and to motivate them to pray for their national leaders. What a great mission!

Besides interceding for lawmakers, the young prayer warriors send notes, letters, and Scriptures they've been praying to leaders in local, state, or national government.

"The only hope for our leaders is Jesus," claims Ashley Austin, age eleven, a California student who joined the National Children's Prayer Network. "If we don't pray, who will? You shouldn't give up praying for our leaders because if you keep trying, you will see a breakthrough in their lives. With God's help and our obedience, righteousness will prevail."

Ashley's school prayed for different leaders in Congress, but her class in particular interceded for its Senator: for her family members, for quality time with family in the midst of her hectic schedule, for her relationships with other leaders and world leaders, for safety in travel, that she would seek God's wisdom, "and things like that."[2] These children firmly believe that "things like that" matter to God, and that He will move on their behalf to change a country and the world.

NETWORKS: A WELL-KEPT SECRET

One of the best-kept secrets I know is the growing presence of children's prayer networks around the world. In Argentina, Australia, New Zealand, South Africa, the United States, Wales, and many other countries, God has been raising up prayer networks of concerned kids. These ministries connect prayer groups from different denominations, churches, races and countries, creating unity and vision for worldwide intercession. They develop "prayer tools" in different languages and equip, disciple, and teach children to pray effectively.

Prayer networks help children become effective prayer warriors in a challenging world. They sponsor conferences and prayer rallies to provide "basic training." And they coordinate with churches, teaching them how to integrate the prayers of children into their congregational life and ministry. These networks especially emphasize intercession, or "pleading in favor of another." They help children learn to listen to God and pray His will—whether it is for a city, a country, or a people group.

Jane Mackie of the Children's Prayer Network of Australia frequently accompanies children on prayer missions. For one outreach, she and her kids joined a forty-hour prayer weekend organized by another ministry, and her group was assigned to pray for a specific country and town. Their assignment was to walk the length of a beach, stand in a certain place, and with a good view of the town across the ocean, pray for the people there.

The only difficulty was the torrential rain. Jane and the other adults borrowed as many umbrellas as they could, dressed the children in plastic garbage bags, and set off on their adventure. The "spot" was now a muddy slope on which the children were slipping and sliding with glee. Because it was too wet to carry books, they had only one Bible available, carried in a pouch around a child's waist.

"With great difficulty I tried to focus the children on the assignment at hand and appealed to them to ask the Lord for a specific

Scripture to pray," recalled Jane. "After a few minutes of silence, four children gave references, not knowing what they were going to mean. Each of them were God's promises we could pray over the town. It became one of our most memorable and exciting moments."

Yes, children's networks are memorable and exciting, especially when they stretch across the globe and potentially shape history.

MILLIONS OF WORLD SHAPERS

The Children's Global Prayer Movement (CGPM), part of the children's track of A.D. 2000, is a good example of how God is uniting children in prayer internationally. The idea for CGPM landed in Esther Ilnisky's heart in 1983 when God showed her His view of children in the 1990s—that they would be graced with a special anointing for prayer. Esther says God impressed on her that children would rise up as a mighty force to intercede on behalf of their generation and for world evangelism.

In 1991, the prayer network took shape when Dr. C. Peter Wagner asked Esther to bring fifty children as praying delegates to the 1995 Global Consultation of World Evangelization. The young delegates were from Argentina, Australia, Brazil, Canada, Fiji, Indonesia, Jamaica, Japan, Korea, Malaysia, and the United States. After contributing to the historic conference, the children returned to their countries and continued to intercede in groups and churches.

The Children's Global Prayer Movement's goal then became to mobilize one million children from all over the world to pray, kids who would pray for children in other nations. Today the movement has already surpassed a million, and the potential for millions of young intercessors is quickly becoming a reality. In Nigeria, 50,000 children who are called "praying firebrands" are part of the CGPM. Argentina and Australia are also key countries in this prayer movement, and the CGPM is presently working with children in thirty nations.

After the children are trained and equipped, they lead prayer in gatherings of major denominations and conferences, and in their churches and schools. And as they pray for children of other nations, God infuses them with His compassion. CGPM kids pray for street children and draw pictures of them. They say very simple prayers for children in war-torn countries, in Muslim nations, and in abusive environments. They also pray for adults who are dealing drugs to kids—to be set free and to stop abusing children. They ask God to send revival and salvation to children around the globe.

"Give the world a hug for Jesus," Esther tells the children. As she teaches and trains young intercessors, their prayers are God's secret weapon for this time in history.

DANIEL PRAYER GROUPS

Wynne Sterns of Kings' Kids, a ministry of Youth With a Mission, started Daniel Prayer Groups (DPG) to mobilize young people in prayer. Gathering kids together in a Daniel Prayer Group takes a variety of forms: weekly groups, day-long or week-long prayer camps, or outreaches on location in a country. Built around active, creative ways of praying, the intercessory groups are linked by the Internet. DPG has its own website with all kinds of prayer tools: ideas for prayer games, instruction on intercession and hearing God, and a country prayer focus for each month.

In 1995, when thousands of adults worldwide were called to pray for the Muslim world during the Islamic month of Ramadan, DPG developed a curriculum called "Hurricane Daniel" that contains creative ideas for a month of prayer for the Muslim world. It included a prayer calendar and suggestions for drama, crafts, relays, and prayer games.

Although the Daniel Prayer Groups started in England, there are DPGs in Canada, Egypt, Norway, Switzerland, the United States, and Papua New Guinea, with more forming each year.

PRAYER NETWORK OF AUSTRALIA AND NEW ZEALAND

Wayne Douglas, coordinator of "Kidzwatch," the Children's Prayer Network of New Zealand, believes God wants to use children and adults in prayer together. "I think the church needs to come together as a whole body—parents, teens, babies, grandparents, children; and as we do, I believe the prophecy of Joel 2, of God pouring out His Spirit, will be fulfilled. I don't think we've experienced anything like what's to come."

Wayne caught this vision when he took children to a five-day Australian National Conference called "Redeeming the Land." At this conference 250 adults and eighty children representing Australia, Canada, Kenya, New Zealand, and the United States united for a time of worship, teaching, and intercession.

During the conference, children learned from the Scriptures, prepared for prayer through adoration and confession, and interceded on behalf of their countries. God brought reconciliation between adults and children, and between participants from New Zealand and Australia. After the children from Kenya sang, the kids prayed for them and for their troubled nation.

The Children's Prayer Networks of Australia and New Zealand seem to be at the forefront of mobilizing children in prayer. In New Zealand, six new groups, started on two islands, participated in the country's first Children's Day of Prayer for the Nation. In Australia, the children have ministered in churches of many different denominations and have built relationships with other cultures—especially the Arabic Christian community, Aboriginal Christians, and Chinese Malaysians.

God opened even more doors of ministry for the Children's Prayer Network. They've been asked to be part of the Olympic Prayer Committee, and have accepted opportunities to travel and minister overseas.

Jane Mackie believes God is doing a mighty work. "I feel God is saying, 'The children are an important part of the Body of Christ; don't leave them out. Don't separate them from real intercession.' Children are an integral part of what God is doing in our time. Those who accept this with humility and welcome them will be blessed."

As Jane, Esther, Wynne, and others speak in churches around the world and disciple children in prayer, they are making a place for kids in God's plan to reach this generation.

A Prayer for the World's Children

Thank You, Lord, that You are calling children
all over our country and around the world to pray.
Thank You for the wonderful people who dedicate their lives
to ministering to and with children.
Thank You for doing more than we could ask
or hope in and through them!

I pray for You to raise up more leaders,

parents, and teachers who are sensitive to Your Spirit

and truly love children.

May they equip and disciple them,

lead and mobilize them in prayer and outreach

—and may You get the glory.

In Jesus' name, Amen.

HELPING KIDS PRAY

Although your children may not be able to travel to Washington on the National Day of Prayer or to another country for an international prayer event, they can participate in special days and times of prayer that affect their country. Here are some ideas:

- *Plan a children's prayer rally.* On the National Day of Prayer, organize a children's prayer rally at a park or government building. Some components of the rally might include a time of worship, a musical performance by a children's choir, breaking into small groups to pray for designated people or topics, and signing a huge banner, with the children's prayers and Scripture verses, to be sent to the appropriate government office.

  A children's prayer rally could be held for other special needs or days such as the Worldwide Day of Prayer for Children at Risk or the Ramadan prayer initiative for the Muslim people.

- *Plan a children's prayer retreat or camp.* Whether it is a one-day retreat or five-day summer intercession camp, setting aside a special time to equip, train, and lead young people in intercession can grow their relationship with God and excite them about prayer. Seek God for specific prayer focuses for the retreat or camp. Recruit a worship leader, seasoned adult intercessors, and college and high school students as trainers and leaders of small groups. Provide times for recreation and fellowship along with practical workshops on such topics as hearing God, letting Scripture guide your prayers, spiritual warfare, and corporate intercession.

- *Connect through cyberspace.* The Internet has many websites and e-mail addresses related to prayer. For example, Child Prayer International is a website specifically focused on prayer for children. There you can receive prayer requests for kids around the world or post a prayer request of your own. Many prayer networks and children's ministry organizations are preparing websites. To find them, type in the name and do a "Search" on the Internet.

- *Connect with a prayer network.* If you want to connect with one of these prayer networks for training, encouragement, or resources, here's how to contact them:

  Children's Global Prayer Movement
  Esther Network International
  854 Conniston Road
  West Palm Beach, FL 33405-2131
  Phone: (561) 832-6490; fax: (561) 832-8043
  Cpgm1992@aol.com

  Children's Prayer Network of Australia
  P. O. Box 470
  Hornsby NSW 2077
  Australia
  Phone: (02) 9457 9889; fax: (02) 9475 0347
  e-mail: jmmackie@ozemail.com.au

  Daniel Prayer Groups
  Youth With a Mission
  11 Fulbar Road
  Paisley PA2 9AW
  Scotland
  Phone: 141-884-8484; fax 141-848-1519
  Website: http://www.ywam.co.uk/dpginter.htm

  Great Commissionary Kids
  1445 Booneville Avenue
  Springfield, MO 65802
  Phone: (417) 862-2781; fax: (417) 862-0503
  Website: The-Great-Commissionary-kids@ag.org

  Kids Pray
  AmeriTribes
  P. O. Box 3717
  Flagstaff, AZ 86003
  Phone: (520) 526-0875; fax (520) 526-0872

  Kidzwatch, Children's Prayer Network of New Zealand
  21 Hurunui St
  Waikanae, New Zealand
  e-mail: w.douglas@xtra.co.nz

  Mrs. Lin Story
  The National Children's Prayer Network
  P. O. Box 9683
  Washington, D. C. 20016

CHAPTER SIXTEEN

Preparing for the Battle

Children today are being born into the "War Zone."
Therefore, we must dress them for spiritual battle
at a very young age.
We cannot wait until they are older...
Satan does not wait for them to mature before he attacks them.

DAVID WALTERS

When thirty-five teenagers at Heath High School in Paduka, Kentucky, bowed their heads to pray on a November morning, no one knew that when they had barely finished saying "Amen," eight of the students would be gunned down. Michael Carneal, a fourteen-year-old freshman opened fire at close range, leaving three students dead, two paralyzed, and three others injured. The entire town of Paduka mourned. We as a nation were shocked.

The Paduka tragedy awakens us to the fact that as Christians, we face spiritual warfare. Three students—Nichole Hadley, Jessica James, and Kayce Stager—became martyrs for their faithful commitment to pray for classmates and the school.

Our children will face spiritual battles too, perhaps not as overt and tragic as what the Paduka students encountered, but warfare nevertheless. As Christian adults who care about our children, we need to deepen their awareness of this fact.

HELPING KIDS BECOME READY

As the outreach team of Mexican and American youth gathered in the square in the middle of the small Mexican rancho, there was little enthusiasm for the heart preparation or prayer that usually preceded their evangelistic events. The leaders realized the ministry time ahead could be difficult, with potential for harassment. This small remote community had a reputation for not only mocking Christians who shared the gospel but also throwing rocks and ice at them. No one knew of a Christian group that had been warmly received by these people.

A few of the teens started to pray, but most in the group acted more like casual observers going through the motions. Suddenly an old woman dressed in black dashed up and began hitting the kids, screaming in anger. Their passivity quickly dissipated. As the woman screamed and cursed, the leaders encouraged the young people to continue in prayer.

Then one team member reminded the rest that they had neglected to put on the "armor of God" and prepare for spiritual warfare through prayer. Quickly the teens began earnestly praying and making movements as if they actually were putting on each piece of armor. As they finished, someone from the village led the screaming woman away.

Later the youth team walked through the streets, knocking on doors and inviting people to their performance. A group of girls encountered the same woman, who again shrieked and tried pulling one of the girls away. Yet the American girl felt no fear. She spoke quietly to the woman, telling her that God loved her. Later someone told the team the woman called herself a witch.

To begin the performance, the kids gathered in the square and began singing songs of praise and worship. Young people, both American and Mexican, shared their testimonies about knowing God through Jesus Christ. At the end of the drama and worship time, they invited the people of the rancho to ask Jesus into their hearts as Lord and Savior. Miraculously, many did.

Hearts in the village people changed that day, but members of the outreach team also gained a new understanding of spiritual warfare and how important it is to prepare for battle. They also learned that with Christ, we need not fear the conflict but can overcome it with confidence in Him.

EQUIPPING OUR YOUNG SAINTS

Few parents would send kids to play competitive football without a helmet and shoulder and knee pads to prevent injuries. In addition to the equipment, we would want the best coaching staff available. The coaches would devise both offensive and defensive strategies, teach our kids to be team members, and make them practice until they knew their plays and techniques well. Good coaches do all they can to prepare players for skirmishes against the "enemy" team.

In a similar way, we shouldn't send our children out to spiritual battle without equipping them with God's armor, significant prayer cover, instruction, and practice in the ministry of prayer.

In a sense, all prayer is spiritual warfare. When we pray for God's kingdom to come on earth as it is in heaven (Matthew 6:10), or for someone to know Christ, we enter enemy territory—Satan's stronghold. "To pray is to be locked in battle with spiritual forces. Spiritual warfare is not a single type of praying. Prayer is warfare," explains Jennifer Dean, author of *The Praying Life*.[1]

But at the same time, the Holy Spirit wields the power to win battles. "God has ordained to dislodge and defeat Satan by the prayers of His people," explains author Wesley Duewel. "The triune God has chosen for the Spirit to empower and pray through you as He indwells and fills you. The Holy Spirit has been charged with the responsibility of engaging in conflict all the power of darkness and reinforcing Christ's victory."[2]

How do we prepare ourselves and our children for these spiritual battles? In 2 Corinthians 10:3–5, Paul explained that instead of rifles and missiles, we are to use spiritual resources: "We are human, but we don't wage war with human plans and methods. We use God's mighty weapons, not merely worldly weapons, to knock down the Devil's strongholds. With these weapons we break down every proud argument that keeps people from knowing God" (NLT).

Jennifer Dean presents a terrific analogy when she advises, "Think of your Spirit-directed prayers as smart bombs landing on enemy strongholds. Your persevering prayers are systematically and precisely destroying Satan's hold." These "smart bombs," computer-driven bombs that hit an exact target, were crucial in America's victory over Iraq in the Gulf War. Similar to these high-tech bombs, our prayers tear down Satan's control over territories in people's lives. That's why the enemy resists our efforts to pray at every turn by confronting us with busyness, discouragement, and other tactics to keep us from invading and driving him out of the territory he has occupied.[3]

Despite Satan's resistance, we can equip our children so their prayers hit the target.

DRESSED FOR BATTLE

Part of our essential weaponry for spiritual battle is the armor of God described in Ephesians 6:11–17. Here Paul advises us to

> Use every piece of God's armor to resist the enemy in the time of evil, so that after the battle you will still be standing firm. Stand your ground, putting on the sturdy belt of truth, the body armor of God's righteousness for shoes, and put on the peace that comes from the Good News, so that you will be fully prepared. In every battle you will need faith as your shield to stop the fiery arrows aimed at you by Satan. Put on salvation as your helmet and take the sword of the Spirit, which is the word of God. (NLT)

This spiritual armor is crucial for intercessors, both young and old. In every battle we need faith as our shield to stop the fiery arrows aimed at us by the enemy. Salvation is our helmet, the assurance of our salvation in Christ that protects us from Satan's lies. We must also take up the sword of the Spirit, which is the Word of God. Jesus, when faced with Satan's attacks in the wilderness, resisted by replying, "It is written..." and quoting His Father's Word. We can respond the same way, reciting Scripture to the enemy of our souls. God has given us His Word as a resource for prayer and for every life situation and spiritual battle we face.

Each of the pieces of armor described in this familiar passage represents our "equipment" for fighting spiritual battles. But they also describe Jesus Christ. He is the "author and finisher" of our faith (Hebrews 12:2, KJV). He is the security of our salvation, and we're clothed in His righteousness (Isaiah 61:10). He is the Living Word, and keeping our minds set on Him unravels Satan's deceptions. He is our peace (Ephesians 2:14), and as we focus on Him, we don't need to fear the enemy. We can pray and live in peace.

So while the armor of God is important, putting it on isn't a ritual we complete before God will hear us; nor is it a lucky rabbit's foot. On the contrary, armor is an excellent word picture to help us understand (and explain to our children) how God has prepared us for spiritual warfare through Jesus Christ, and that all we need is to abide *in Christ*. When we clothe ourselves in Christ—focusing on and trusting in Him—we're prepared for battle!

Still, there are other weapons in the spiritual arsenal that we and our children can use to stand firm against the enemy.

PROVIDING A PRAYER COVER

Much as air force or navy jets provide air cover for an impending military maneuver, we parents provide a "prayer cover" for our children's spiritual and physical protection as we intercede for them daily. In a sense, through prayer, we dress our kids for battle.

Ben Strong, the seventeen-year-old leader of the Heath High School prayer group in Paduka, is a vivid example of the importance of prayer cover. Though people at his church didn't know what lay ahead, Ben was the focus of much prayer the night before the gun-shooting tragedy. After the church's evening service, Ben's mom, Doris, felt unsettled and asked if those present would join hands and pray for her son. As the group interceded, a man placed his hands on Ben's shoulders and prayed for the teen's safety.

"Lord, give him protection!" he cried out. "Protection, protection," he said over and over as he prayed for God to send angels to surround and guard Ben.

The next morning after the initial blasts from Michael's gun, Ben bravely risked his life and intervened. He walked up to Michael, took the smoking 22-caliber semi-automatic pistol from his hand and said, "Michael, stop! What are you doing?" Ignoring Michael's plea to shoot him, Ben took his classmate to the principal's office down the hall.[4]

God's work in the midst of this senseless tragedy is still unfolding. The Heath High School prayer group has grown from the initial thirty-five to more than 250 students who meet to pray for their school every morning.

"These kids are fervent in their prayers now. They know they're making a stand and that it can be dangerous to pray," says Georgia Tomlin, an English teacher at the high school.[5] Inspired by the faith of these students, new prayer groups have sprung up in high schools across the country. Observing the love and forgiveness of the victims' families, more than 100 teenagers and adults have committed their lives to Christ. Millions of people witnessed the gospel's influence when CNN aired the memorial services of Nichole, Jessica, and Kayce.

"Pray in the Spirit on all occasions with all kinds of prayers and requests. With this in mind, be alert and always keep on praying for all the saints," says Ephesians 6:18. More than ever, we need to support our children and teens. We need to pray for them *at all times and seasons* of their lives. There is never a time they don't need our prayer cover. We can pray for them on *every occasion* and about everything that concerns them. We're to "stay alert and watch with strong purpose" (AMP), and be persistent in our prayers, persevering in intercession because our kids face intense spiritual opposition in almost every corner of their world.

"It's a war out there; we face so many temptations, so much pressure and spiritual battles every day," said a Christian student I talked with recently. "To be a shining lamp for Jesus takes twice as much oil because the battle is so intense!" However, we aren't the only ones who can wage war and provide a spiritual cover for kids. Our children can also pray a cover over one another. Young ones can pray, "Lord, help my friend Melissa," while teens can pray more specifically against Satan's onslaughts. As they pray for one another, they help fulfill the need for prayer cover in spiritual battle. After all, God has called together an army, not lone soldiers.

BRINGING IN THE REINFORCEMENTS

When our first granddaughter, Caitlin, was born recently, we were poignantly reminded of the need for unity and agreement in prayer, especially during times of crisis. Born a month early with the umbilical cord wrapped around her neck and fluid aspirated into her lungs, Caitlin wasn't breathing. Even after the doctor administered oxygen, she suffered severe respiratory distress. By the next morning Caitlin was in critical condition, and doctors transported her to a neonatal intensive care unit (NICU) at another hospital.

The doctors called her "a fighter," and her courageous spirit struggled for life as the medical team labored. But even with a ventilator, an oscillator, blood transfusions and medication, all we heard for forty-eight hours was, "Still critical...next few days will tell...wait and see."

Instead of just waiting, we decided to "wait and pray." The Lord reminded me of the miraculous recoveries of two critically ill children I had written about in my book *When Mothers Pray,* and the influence of a large network of intercessors on their behalf. He prompted me to call others to join our family in praying for Caitlin. We contacted churches and prayer chains, who in turn called others. Moms In Touch International asked their state coordinators around the United States to pray. Soon a huge prayer team stretched from Oklahoma to Florida, Colorado to California, and around the globe to Germany, where a missionary kids' school and the Children's Prayer Networks of New Zealand and Australia joined in prayer on behalf of Caitlin.

Little voices and big ones, childlike prayers and mature ones, God heard Caitlin Elizabeth's name over and over! When doctors saw a change and warned, "This is not going well; this is what needs to happen to Caitlin's lungs," we passed that request to the intercessors. Twice a day a mother from our College Moms In Touch group relayed the newest prayer requests.

As we waited for Caitlin, our family also prayed for the twenty-three babies in the NICU with her, and for peace for their worried parents. As several of the babies rallied and went home, we rejoiced with their parents and thanked God as we continued praying for Caitlin's turnaround. We also requested more prayer for the nighttime because she seemed to suffer setbacks during those hours.

Finally, on Thursday night of the second week, Caitlin improved. In fact, a doctor said her X-ray on Friday morning looked like different lungs than the ones he examined on Thursday. Prayers continued as she transferred from the ventilator to an oxygen "space helmet" and began the difficult task of breathing on her own. After another week, her lungs recovered enough to breathe without extra oxygen.

As I write this, Caitlin is now home with her parents and delighting us all. Yet I wonder if her life would have been possible if we hadn't called in the prayer reinforcements. Through that crisis, we learned more about waging warfare together, and the importance of giving God precise requests. For example, when Caitlin was taking eighty to one hundred breaths per minute, we prayed for her respiration to drop to between forty and sixty breaths per minute. And we specifically thanked and praised God when her breathing slowed down.

Children around the world were part of Caitlin's prayer cover, and I know God used our situation to help them realize both His awesome power and the need to "bring in reinforcements" for whatever needs they may face in the future. Through real-life situations such as Caitlin's, we can teach children to ask family, friends, teachers, and church members to help wage the spiritual battle and win.

PRAISING AND DRAWING NEAR TO GOD

"From the lips of children and infants you have ordained praise because of your enemies, to silence the foe and the avenger" (Psalm 8:2).

Scripture is clear that the praise and worship of young children defeats Satan and his schemes. God inhabits the praise of His children (Psalm 22:3) and leads them into victory. In spiritual battle, we dare not underestimate the value of praise or neglect teaching its value to our kids.

Children don't understand all of the theology behind praise, but they can grasp its significance. When children from the Kidzwatch Prayer Network of New Zealand praised, worshiped, and marched on a map of their country, it wasn't just a game. They were proclaiming Jesus Christ's lordship over their country, hoping and praying for a spiritual breakthrough for New Zealand as they marched.

We also prepare children for spiritual battle through the regular practice of confession. James told believers, "Resist the devil [stand firm against him] and he will flee from you. Come near to God and he will come near to you. Wash your hands, you sinners, and purify your hearts..." (James 4:7–8).

We draw close to God whenever we ask Him to search our hearts and spotlight anything we've said, done, or thought that has grieved the Holy Spirit. This "heart cleansing" positions young prayer warriors for battle by shutting the door to Satan's influence and relying on the Holy Spirit to guide and empower them.

Joyce Satter, who has worked with children and youth for many years, suggests that we tell kids, "We don't want this prayer time to be influenced by the enemy so we pray, 'Satan, in the name of Jesus, I tell you to go away. You have no part in this prayer time.'" (See James 4:7.) While avoiding too much emphasis on the devil, it's a simple way to tell him, "Get lost!" With the enemy banished from the prayer circle, kids can now yield their thoughts, prayers, and actions to God's Holy Spirit.

WORDS OF CAUTION

Any discussion of spiritual warfare and children needs a few words of caution. I don't advocate sending kids into major spiritual battlefields in which they intentionally confront the evil principalities and powers of this dark world. It's not wise to thrust children into battles they aren't prepared to fight. Confronting and binding principalities and powers shouldn't be engaged in lightly by adults, much less kids.

However, if during prayer time a child says of his own initiative, "I think the Lord is showing me that He's weeping over the sins of our city and wants me to pray," that is different from imposing warfare on him. We should *not* be telling impressionable and often fearful young children, "There are lots of lost, sinful people trapped in darkness in our city and we're going to do spiritual warfare and come against the ruling dark powers." Teaching children about spiritual warfare is an age-sensitive matter that must take into consideration their individual readiness and personalities. Know the children, discern God's heart for them, and be led by His Spirit. Be obedient to how God directs you and the children in your charge.

"It's not like building a model airplane," says Jerry Lenz, a Toronto children's pastor. "There aren't pat answers or 1-2-3 formulas for this in Scripture." Jerry says a ten-year-old boy in a group may be ready for engaging in spiritual warfare and desire to intercede for a nation, while a fourteen year old in the same group may not be.

Be sure it's the Holy Spirit who is drawing the children and leading their prayer time, so they don't just parrot spiritual warfare jargon they've heard from adults. And especially don't pressure them to perform. As you keep asking, seeking, and knocking, the Holy Spirit will give kids a burden to pray for certain things. He's the best teacher!

Most of all, encourage children with the fact that God is great, and He's in charge of their lives and the world. We know that "the one who is in you is greater [even if you are a child] than the one [Satan] who is in the world" (1 John 4:4). Although God uses human vessels to pray and minister, *the battle is the Lord's.* Better yet, He's already won the war! Satan's forces were defeated at the cross. Colossians 2:15 explains, "Having disarmed the powers and authorities, he made a public spectacle of them, triumphing over them by the cross."

No matter the circumstances, God is in control, and this can reassure people of all ages. As we look to Him for marching orders in the spiritual battle, He will lead us and our children from glory to glory and victory to victory.

A Prayer for the Spiritual Battle

Lord, I thank You that You are the Victor,
that You are sovereign over all the earth.
Thank You that You grant us the privilege
of partnering with You in Your purpose
to advance Your kingdom, set the captives free,
and stand against the forces of darkness.
Thank You that You are our refuge and strength!
Grant me the alertness and grace to be persistent
and faithful in prayer for my children and all children.
Send Your Holy Spirit to guide me to pray in wisdom and power
and to lead our children as we stand in intercessory prayer
before Your throne.
Send Your angels to protect them and
give us courage and dependence upon You!
In Jesus' name, Amen.

HELPING KIDS PRAY

In a recent article in *Pray!* magazine titled "Families Under Attack," Tom White suggests that in view of the spiritual battle, our homes need to be places of refuge and peace for children. How can our homes become a spiritual refuge? How can we deal with the enemy's assaults from within and without? Tom offers these excellent ideas.

- *Seek God's protection.* "In vigilant prayer, we can ask God that the place where we dwell would become a reservoir of life and hope for all who cross our threshold," Tom says. It begins by setting our home apart for God's use with a simple prayer and declaration: "As for me and my house, we will serve the LORD!" (Joshua 24:15). As we invite His presence into our home daily, and rid the house of ungodly things that pollute us and our children's lives, it becomes a "perimeter of God's protection."

- *Set aside places and times for Jesus in family life.* Throughout this book, we've looked at creative ways to "seek first His kingdom" (Matthew 6:33) by sharing in God's Word, praise and worship, and intercession with the family. "Seeking the kingdom" is one of the best strategies to maintain God's peace and protection and defeat Satan. White says, "A chief tactic of the enemy is to rob us of our confidence in God's ability to strengthen us through the joy of His Son and Spirit. We must regularly close doors on doubt and discouragement and open doors for the King of Glory to enter our hearts and homes."

- *Learn to discern.* Knowing how to stand on and speak biblical truth, to walk in forgiveness, and to discern the enemy's influences is an important part of spiritual warfare. Tom suggests applying the name and blood of Jesus to overcome enemy influences (Revelation 12:10–11), to ask God for helping angels (Psalm 91, Hebrews 1:14), and to apply Ephesians 6:16–18: "Pray at all times [on every occasion, in every season] in the Spirit, with all [manner of] prayer and entreaty. To that end keep alert and watch with strong purpose and perseverance, interceding in behalf of all the saints" (AMP).[6]

Dear God,
Thank you for my family. Thank you for helping my grandma be healthy.
Please help all my friends become Christians!

—Clayton, 9

dear lord jesus.
i have a burden on my heart. you know that i only want to do
your will and steer away from things that would pull me away
from you. this includes dating and guys i only want to date the
guy you'd want me to (ultimately to wait for my future
husband!) i really pray that you would put a hedge of protection
that i can sense around me and give me discernment. make
me strong and confident in you and guide me in what to say.
thank you so much for listening.
i love you.

—Alisha, 13

CHAPTER SEVENTEEN

Opening Up the Prayer Closet

God wants to use children. He wants to reveal Himself
to them and move through them.
We must forever reject the idea that children
should sit on the sidelines when God is at work.

DAVID WALTERS

When Shirley Launcelot was diagnosed with breast cancer and faced surgery, chemotherapy, and radiation treatments, many church members prayed for her recovery. But Shirley experienced some of her most significant prayer support from the 400 children she pastored at a Fort Worth, Texas, church.

After the children heard about her battle with cancer, they told their Sunday school teachers they wanted to pray for "Miss Shirley" and went to work on their knees. But soon they returned to their leaders and said, "Tell us specific ways we can pray."

Instead of thinking she might burden the kids, Shirley recognized an ideal way to help the children learn the fundamentals of prayer.

"We took the kids seriously and seized the opportunity to show them that when you pray specifically, God answers specifically," says Shirley.

The children received weekly updates and prayer requests, and from the beginning of Shirley's treatment they saw God's answers. They prayed that she wouldn't get sick from chemotherapy or radiation so she could continue to minister at the church; in nine months of aggressive cancer treatment, Shirley never missed a day of work. She never experienced the usual severe nausea and vomiting. Tiredness, yes. But except for the surgery, Shirley never was so flattened that she couldn't continue in her job.

While taking radiation treatments, Shirley had to drive from Fort Worth to a Dallas hospital on thirty-two different days. Since the highway was torn up and construction delays were common, the children prayed for clear roads, no traffic problems, and no rain during Miss Shirley's drive from the church to the hospital and back.

For every one of her thirty-two treatments, the roads and highways were clear to travel, with no delays or problems. The weather was pleasant except for one day when the sky was pouring rain and the news stations announced flash flood warnings. However, when Shirley left the church to drive to Dallas, the rain suddenly stopped. As she drove, the sun shone brightly; when she pulled into the church's driveway later, it started raining again. The children cheered and clapped the next Sunday when they heard how their prayers had been answered.

Some kids took on specific needs to address in prayer. For example, five-year-old Michael was concerned about Shirley's hair falling out, so he mounted his own campaign for her hair to grow back quickly. Every day he reminded his parents and siblings to pray for Miss Shirley's hair. When he saw her at church, he asked, "Do you have any hair yet?"

Shirley updated Michael about the new growth: a half-inch, then an inch, then two. And finally, when her hair had grown out enough, he was the first child to see her without a wig. Michael beamed when he saw that God had not only answered his prayers, but He had done more than asked. Miss Shirley's hair hadn't just grown back; the new hair was thicker and healthier than ever before.

THE BLESSING OF INTERGENERATIONAL PRAYER

On Tuesday nights at the Houston House of Prayer, youth are encouraged to attend the prayer meeting along with the adults. Darla Ryden, who guides the youth, feels it is important for youth to learn prayer from the adults, and that young people can contribute significantly to the prayer meeting. From time to time she asks the kids what they're hearing from God and encourages them to share it.

One night during the meeting, Dan, a junior higher, felt burdened for his school. As he shared his concerns about spiritually lost students and the need for God to transform teachers and kids, the adults decided to pray for the community's schools. Those prayers began a ripple effect. A girl from Dan's school began praying with him and they decided to keep meeting regularly. Other children and teens from the church started interceding for their schools. Parents prayed for their children's classmates, teachers, and principals. Because one young man shared his concern, adults and youth united in prayer. Today the intercession continues, taking on different forms as new people catch the vision to pray for their schools.

In other places, ministry leaders have discovered that when they open up the prayer closet and "make room for the children," a blessing is sure to follow.

In Ventura County, California, a concert of prayer meets every month on Sunday evenings. Anywhere from 25 to 600 adults from a variety of denominations, along with four to ten children, join together to intercede for their community. Adults who hear the children pray just melt, amazed at their insight and passion. A seven-year-old boy prays his heart out, burdened for the spiritually lost in Ventura. A nine-year-old girl prays, "Lord, You're excellent! You're powerful! Bring all these people in crack houses and our neighborhood to know you! Free them from addiction! Lord, please clean the hearts of the police!"

This is the power of intergenerational prayer: children and adults believing God together, learning from one another and reaping the joyful results.

HOW TO OPEN THE PRAYER CLOSET

How can we make room for the children and welcome them in our prayer meetings and events? Here are some tips for bringing children into intergenerational services, house church meetings, or small groups—anytime adults and children can pray together.[1]

• *Shorten and simplify the prayers.* Children have shorter attention spans than adults and feel easily intimidated by eloquent, long prayers. So try simple, one-sentence prayers. This encourages children to think, I could do that! I could join in and pray. God isn't impressed with long-windedness, so when you're praying with kids, keep the requests and prayers short and they'll be more apt to pray aloud. (Quiet, shy adults will participate more too!)

You'll also find it helpful to break the prayer session into topics. You could divide the children and adults into small groups and call out a new prayer target about every five to eight minutes.

• *Make prayer time God-focused.* Fawn Parish, coordinator for the Ventura County Concerts of Prayer and mother of a nine year old, says the weight of any prayer burden should be balanced by the power and excellency of God. When we're praying about needy or sad situations—abused children, homeless people, or a nation in darkness—it's easy to fall into worldly sorrow, which leads to despair. Over time this sadness leads to prayer burnout. So whenever we pray, and especially when we pray with children, we need to keep the focus on God. No matter how big the need is, God's mercy, greatness, love, sovereignty, and power are greater!

"When God is your focus and the Bible is your prayer book, then kids don't get burned out or heavy-hearted from intercession," Fawn says.

Not long ago, when Fawn picked up her son Joel from school, he said, "I prayed for all my friends on the playground today, and especially Josh." Later at dinner he explained. "Joshua [a seven-year-old classmate] wants to commit suicide because his dad is beating his mom and he has to watch. He can't stand it, so he wants to die. But he wants to live because of his little sister."

When they joined hands to pray for Joshua, Fawn prayed, "God, Your heart is to let the little children come to You. You are so merciful and loving! You weep when little kids like Josh are in pain. Jesus, would You be Joshua's friend, comfort him and keep him safe, and heal the source of the problem? Would You cause his parents to become godly parents and give them friends who know and love You?"

Keeping the focus on God's goodness helped Joel not be overly burdened by his friend's problems.

• *Add some fun!* You can make prayer time exciting with many of the activities already described in this book. Remember that prayer times don't have to be "all work and no play." Kids transition easily from the "seriousness" of prayer into the fun of play and laughter. So if you lead children and adults on a prayer walk, also stop by a playground to hop on the swings or visit an ice cream shop.

Let children see that prayer is a great adventure—that there's no place in the world they can't touch through prayer. Kids love to be a part of something bigger than themselves, and they'll find it exciting to partner with God through prayer!

• *Explain that God loves to hear their voices.* I shared with our Children's Church group that when my college kids lived on campus, miles away from home, I missed them. I could barely wait for them to call. When they did, I dropped everything, thrilled to hear their voices! God feels that way about His children, only thousands of times more. As we adults show we're pleased with the sound of kids' voices in prayer, they'll feel more assured that God is too.

Also, assure children that God wants to speak to them. Ask them what Scriptures come to mind as they pray about a subject, or if there is a picture God seems to be impressing them to share. Their impressions can further direct prayer and encourage them that they're growing as prayer warriors.

• *Let the children pray what is on their hearts.* One child may always be burdened for the poor or the disabled. Another may feel deeply about a specific country or want to pray frequently about an issue. Even though it's not the prayer target for the group, make room for them to pray about their burden, and join in.

• *Bless the children as pray-ers.* One Sunday at our church, a team of fifteen intercessors joined the kids in Children's church. After Kathleen, the leader, shared some thoughts about intercession, the adults spread throughout the room, two or three to a group of children. The adults prayed with the kids for the church, our city, our nation, and the president. They also prayed special blessings on each child.

The adults encouraged the kids to share what God spoke to them and affirmed them as pray-ers. Then they invited the children to join the ministry teams at the front of the sanctuary during an upcoming service. The kids loved the adult attention and couldn't wait to be included in the ministry time. Affirmation by the adult intercessors made the children feel that their contribution of prayer was of significant value to the kingdom.

• *Share prayer needs with them.* Don't leave kids out of the prayer loop—give them prayer requests just as you would adults. When you plan a special prayer project, invite the children and youth, letting them know their presence and prayers are important.

You'll find, as I have, that children can be astounding prayer partners. They will surprise you with their spiritual insights, amaze you with their big hearts, encourage you when they pray for your needs, humble you with their great faith in God, and challenge you to spend more time on your knees.

I pray God will increase your vision for how He wants to use children in prayer. I pray that He will increase your faith—and the faith of your kids—as you see Him work! May you and your children grow in the grace of our Lord Jesus Christ, experiencing His presence more and more. May you equip them to fulfill the calling and destiny God has for their lives and this generation. And may you discover the awesome, wonderful things God does when children pray.

A Prayer for the Church

Heavenly Father,
You've called Your church to be a house of prayer,
filled with people who devote themselves to intercession.
Thank You for the spirit of prayer that
You are pouring out on the church in our time.
But let us not forget the children and youth in our prayer gatherings!
Show us how to include them
so they can rise up as ministering members of the Body of Christ,
fulfilling Your plans and purposes.
In Jesus' name, Amen.

HELPING KIDS PRAY

Throughout this book we've explored different ways to pray with children. Now ask yourself some questions to help put these ideas to work.

• Are there prayer events in your church or community in which both you and your child could participate? If so, what are they? Or how could you begin an adult/child prayer group?

- Think of your kids' gifts and learning styles. What are specific, creative ways you could pray with them to align with their individual bents?
- How, specifically, can you initiate or improve group prayer in your family?
- What promises of God will you begin praying for your kids? Claim a specific Scripture verse for each child. Why did you choose the verses you did?
- What do each of your kids need to learn about spiritual warfare? How can you teach them?

RECOMMENDED RESOURCES

BOOKS AND PUBLICATIONS

- Bradley, Ed. *Cry of the City.* Monthly prayer guide for interceding for street children in megacities. Oakseed Ministries, P.O. Box 11222, Burke, VA 22009. Website: www.oakseed.org or E-mail: oakseeds@aol.com.
- Brown, Julie. *Kids Pray Resource Handbook.* AmeriTribes, P. O. Box 3717, Flagstaff, AZ 86003. (520) 526-0875 phone; (520) 526-0872 fax.
- *Children of the Window Prayer Calendar.* Caleb Project, 10 W. Dr. Creek Circle, Littleton, CO 80210. E-mail: info@cproject.com; Website:www.calebproject.org.
- *Children's 30-Day Muslim Prayer Guide.* World Christian News & Books, P.O. Box 264791, Colorado Springs, CO 80936. E-mail: wcn@xc.org.
- Cloyd, Betty Shannon. *Children and Prayer: A Shared Pilgrimage.* Upper Room Books, 1997.
- Coleman, Robert and A. Duane Litfin. *Accounts of a Campus Revival: Wheaton College, 1995.* Harold Shaw Publishers, 1995.
- Dobson, Shirley, and Pat Verbal. *My Family's Prayer Calendar.* Ministry to Today's Child, 2836 Summer Brooke Way, Casselberry, FL 32707. Order from (800) 406-1011. Also available in Christian bookstores.
- Esther Network International. *Children's Global Prayer Movement: What about the Children?* Also prayer calendars, *PRAY USA! Prayer Calendar for Kids,* Prayer Spinner, "House of Prayer" audio tape, and Global "Catch the Vision" soft globe of the world to make an impression and impact on the world by prayer. Esther Network International, 854 Conniston Road, West Palm Beach, FL 33405-2131.
- Fuller, Cheri. *When Mothers Pray.* Multnomah Publishers, 1997.
- Harris, Jill and Bob Sjogren. *The Teacher's Manual for the Destination 2000 and Teacher's Training Video Curriculum.* Frontiers, 325 N. Stapley Drive, Mesa, Arizona 85203. (602) 834-1500.
- Henly, Karyn. *Child-Sensitive Teaching: Helping Children Grow a Living Faith in a Loving God.* Standard Publishing, 1997.
- Higgs, Mike. *The Campus Prayer Handbook for Students.* Canby, OR: CityLINC Resources, 1997. Order from LINC Ministries, P. O. Box 922, Canby, OR 97013. (403) 266-9914. E-mail: lincministries@compuserve.com.

- Hohmann, Pete. *The Great Commissionary Kids Intensive Care Unit: Mobilizing Kids for Outreach.* Published by Boys & Girls Missionary Crusade, 1997. (417) 862-2781 phone; (417) 862-0503 fax. Website: The-Great-Commissionary-Kids@ag.org.
- How to Start a Children's Prayer Ministry. An inspirational booklet and tape sharing true stories and how-to ideas to begin an exciting prayer ministry in your church or school. Available from Ministry to Today's Child, 2836 Summer Brooke Way, Casselberry, FL 32707. (800) 406-1011. E-mail: MTTC@aol.com.
- *Hurricane Daniel and Daniel Prayer Groups Package.* YWAM, 11 Fulbar Road, Paisley, PA2 9AW, Scotland, 141-887-8584 phone; 141-848-1519 fax. Website: www.ywam.dpgpray.htm.
- Johnstone, Jill. *You Can Change the World, Volumes 1 and 2.* Zondervan Publishing.
- Johnstone, Patrick. *Operation World.* Available at Christian bookstores or by writing YWAM Publishing, P.O. Box 95787, Seattle, WA 98155.
- Kilbourn, Phyllis. *Children In Crisis: A New Commitment.* Marc Publications.
- World Vision International. 121 E. Huntington Dr. Monrovia, CA 91016-3400.
- Layton, Dian. *Soldiers With Little Feet: Preparing Our Children for His Presence.* Shippensburg, PA: Destiny Image, 1996.
- Lewis, Karen and Alice Erath Roder. *From Arapesh to Zuni: A Book of Bibleless Peoples.* Wycliffe Bible Translators, P.O. Box 2727, Huntington Beach, CA 92647-0727.
- Mackie, Jane. *Kids Pray!* Available from Children's Prayer Network of Australia, P.O. Box 470 Hornsby, NSO 2077, Australia (02) 9457 9889 phone; (02) 9489 5323 fax. E-mail: jmmackie@ozemail.com.au. Or from Peacemakers Ministries, P.O. Box 600, Cootamundra, NSW 2590.
- MemLok Bible Memory System. An illustrated Bible memory system for families. 420 E. Montwood Ave, La Habra, CA 90631. (800) 373-1947.
- Merritt, Jan. *Prayer Kids Notebook.* 47 Ravenwood Circle, Bloomington, IL 61704. E-mail: PRAYKIDS@aol.com.
- *Tracking Your Walk.* Prayer diary for youth. YWAM Publishing, P.O. Box 95787, Seattle, WA 98155 or at Christian bookstores.
- Verbal, Pat. *Action Keys to Prayer.* Curriculum of eight reproducible Bible studies on prayer for 8 to 12-year-olds, including skits, games and activities adaptable to any size group. Also, Obie's Bible Prayer Overheads. Twelve colorful prayers on overhead transparencies that teach children to pray like Moses, Daniel, Paul, and Jesus, and other Bible characters. Includes discussion questions.

- Walters, David. *Children Aflame, Kids In Combat, Equipping the Younger Saints.* Available from Good News Ministries. 220 Sleepy Creek Road, Macon, GA 31210. (912) 757-8071.
- Worldwide Day of Prayer for Children at Risk information pack. Viva Network, P.O. Box 633, Oxford, OX2 OXZ, U.K. +44 1865 450800 phone; +44 1865 203567 fax. E-mail: prayer@viva.org.
- 10/40 Window Fact Sheet. Helpful tool in praying for the Muslim countries. Available from Kids Can Make a Difference, 4445 Webster Drive, York, PA 17402.

VIDEOS

- *Generation.* A video about how God is using youth around the world in evangelism, prayer, and missions. Mars Hills Productions, 12705 S. Kirkwood, Suite 218, Stafford, TX 77477 (800) 580-6479. http://www.mars-hill-media.org.
- *Mobilizing Kids for Ministry.* Great Commissionary Kids video. Helps teachers and children's ministry leaders develop missions education for children. The Great Commissionary Kids, 1445 Boonville Avenue, Springfield, MO 65802. (417) 862-2781, ext. 4009.
- *Moms In Touch International.* A video that helps mothers catch a vision for what God can do when we pray for our children and schools. Moms In Touch International, P. O. Box 1120, Poway, CA 92074-1120. 1-800-949-MOMS.
- *Prayerwalking for Kids.* Helps children catch the vision for prayer walking in their communities and how all of life can be a visual aid for prayer. Joey and Fawn Parish, 540 W. Highland Drive, Camarillo, CA 93010. (805) 987-0064.
- "See You at the Pole." A prayer movement that began with a few students and spread to millions around the United States and the world. Video describes the largest student prayer gathering in history. See You at the Pole, P.O. Box 60134, Fort Worth, TX 76115. (817) 447-7526. www.SYATP.com.
- *Step by Step: Leading Your Child to Christ.* Art Murphy from Arrow Ministries. An 85-minute video for parents and teachers, a 60-minute audio cassette for church staff, and/or a 3.5" computer disk. "Step by Step" shares Art's understanding of helping children come to know the Lord and how to set them on the right track toward discipleship so they mature in Christ. Arrow Ministries, P. O. Box 568554, Orlando, FL 32856-8554. (407) 859-9683.
- *Teachers' Training Curriculum.* Destination 2000 Videos, a ministry of Frontiers. Learn how to teach missions to children in an exciting, fun-packed way. Frontiers, 325 N. Stapley Drive, Mesa, Arizona 85203. (602) 834-1500.

- *Tell Me about God: Helping Children Develop a Relationship with God.* Paraclete Press, P. O. Box 1568, Orleans, MA 02653. (800) 451-5006 or www.paraclete-press.com.
- *The 10/40 Window for Children.* Focuses children on praying for the unreached people groups in the 10/40 Window. Joey and Fawn Parish, 540 W. Highland Drive, Camarillo, CA 93010. (805) 987-0064.
- *To the Ends of the Earth: Praying Through the Window.* An A.D. 2000 video that opens your eyes to God's plan for His majesty to be revealed to the ends of the earth. Christian Information Network, 11025 State Highway 83, Colorado Springs, CO 80921. (719) 522-1040 phone; 548-9000 fax.

WEBSITES AND INTERNET RESOURCES

- Children's Prayer Network of Australia. jmmackie@ozemail.com.au.
- Christian Information Network. Information on praying through the 10/40 Window. www.christian-info.com.
- Daniel Prayer Groups. www.ywam.co.uk.
- Global Prayer Digest. Information on praying for unreached peoples. E-mail a message to hub@xc.org saying "subscribe brigada-pubs-globalprayer digest".
- Great Commissionary Kids. The-Great-Commissionary-Kids@ag.org.
- Harris, Jill. Children's Mission Specialist at Advancing Churches In Missions Commitment. jill.harris@juno.com.
- Kidszwatch. Children's Prayer Network of New Zealand. w.douglas@xtra.co.nz.
- Link International. Newsletter for children about praying for persecuted Christians around the world. www.linkingup.com.
- Viva Network. Worldwide Day of Prayer for Children at Risk. Prayer@viva.org.
- 21st Century Kids Connect. A network to connect children's ministry leaders, kids to kids, kids to culture, and kids to Christ. 21stKidsConnect@xc.org.

NOTES

INTRODUCTION

1. E. M. Bounds, *Prayer and Praying Men* (Grand Rapids: Baker Book House, 1991), 60.

CHAPTER ONE: THE POWER OF YOUTHFUL PRAYERS

1. Jane Mackie, ed. *Kids' Konnection, The Newsletter of the Children's Prayer Network of Australia,* No. 7 (July 1997), 3.
2. Wesley Stafford in foreword to Phyllis Kilbourn, *Children in Crisis* (Monrovia, CA: MARC, World Vision International, 1996), iii.
3. Ibid., 1.
4. Ibid., 1.
5. "The Status of Abortion in America," Information Sheet from Focus on the Family based on the Centers for Disease Control and Prevention's (CDC) *Abortion Surveillance Report* (May 1996), 1.
6. Dan Coats, "America's Youth: A Crisis of Character," *IMPRIMIS* 20, NO. 9 (September 1991), 1.
7. Ibid., 1.
8. David Bryant, "God Is Up to Something!" *Pray!,* Issue 1 (1997), 14.
9. Ibid., 14.
10. Ibid., 14–15.
11. From interview with Esther Ilniskky, who led a children's prayer emphasis at the 1995 Global Congress on World Evangelization in Seoul, Korea.

CHAPTER TWO: THE MIRACLE OF CHILDLIKE FAITH

1. From a message by Chuck Pierce, adapted from *Possessing Your Inheritance,* to be released by Regal Books in 1998. Used by permission.
2. Adapted from Brenda Steen's "God's Secret Weapon," *Winner's Way* (January 1996), and a message entitled "Jesus Loves the Little Children," delivered at the November 17, 1995 Prayer Conference, Living Word Christian Center, Minneapolis, MN.
3. Gloria Gaither, quoted in *Draper's Book of Quotations for the Christian World* (Wheaton: Tyndale House Publishers, 1992), 62.
4. From *Pen Power* (May 1995), published by Chisholm Elementary School, Edmond, Oklahoma.
5. From an interview with Pete Hohmann and his account in *The Great Commissionary Kids Intensive Care Unit* (Mechanicsville, VA: Boys and Girls Missionary Crusade, 1997), 9–10.
6. Mattie Mallory, *Purity Journal,* Volume 1 (July 1904–June 1905).
7. Alice Smith, *Beyond the Veil* (Houston: SpinTruth, 1996), 90–91.
8. Alan D. Wright, *A Chance at Childhood Again* (Sisters, OR: Multnomah Publishers, 1997).

CHAPTER THREE: CHANGING OUR MINDS ABOUT KIDS

1. Sharon Begley, "How to Build a Baby's Brain," *Newsweek* Special Issue, "Your Child" (Spring/Summer 1997), 28–32.
2. E. M. Bounds, *Prayer and Praying Men* (Grand Rapids: Baker Book House, 1991), 59–60.
3. David Walters, *Children Aflame* (Taylors, S.C.: Faith Printing Company, 1995), 22.
4. Ibid., 29.
5. Ibid., 26.
6. *Generation Personal Study Guide* (Stafford, TX: Mars Hill Productions, Inc., 1997), 8.
7. Jill Johnstone, *You Can Change the World* (Grand Rapids: Zondervan Publishing House, 1992), 6.
8. See Recommended Resources for ordering information for "My Family's Prayer Calendar" and other prayer resources to use with children published by Ministry to Today's Child.
9. Johnstone, 6, 8–9.

CHAPTER FOUR: PRAYING PARENTS, PRAYING KIDS

1. Dr. Howard G. Hendricks, quoted by Reg Grant in "Learning to Teach," *Discipleship Journal*, Issue 82 (1994), 35.
2. "The National Assessment of Education Progress Report," reported in *What Works: Research about Teaching and Learning* (Washington, D.C.: United States Department of Education, 1986), 15.
3. V. Gilbert Beers, "Teaching Children to Pray," *Parents & Children* (Colorado Springs: Victor Books, 1986), 668.
4. Gerald Regier, "Being a Consistent Model," *Parents & Children* (Colorado Springs: Victor Books, 1986), 588.
5. Corrie ten Boom with C. C. Carlson, *In My Father's House* (Grand Rapids: Fleming H. Revell Company, 1976), 66.
6. Alice Smith, *Beyond the Veil* (Houston: SpiriTruth Publishing, 1996), 70.
7. Francois Fénélon, *Talking with God* (Brewster, MA: Paraclete Press, 1997), 6.

CHAPTER FIVE: WHO IS GOD AND IS HE LISTENING?

1. Ramona Cramer Tucker, ed., *Little Minds with Big Hearts* (Chicago: Moody Press, 1996), 36.
2. Karyn Henley, *Child-Sensitive Teaching* (Cincinnati: Standard Publishing, 1997), 32.
3. Ibid., 33.
4. Corrie ten Boom, *In My Father's House* (Grand Rapids: Fleming H. Revell Company, 1976), 23–24.
5. ten Boom, 24.
6. Art Murphy, "Step By Step: Leading Your Child to Christ." Video. (Orlando, FL: Arrow Ministries). See Recommended Resources for more information.
7. Roberta Hromas and Todd Temple, *Teaching Your Child to Talk to God* (New York: Inspirational Press, 1994, in arrangement with Thomas Nelson Publishers, 1994), 108–109.
8. Charles Spurgeon, *Prayer Portions for Daily Living* (Chicago: Moody Press, 1978), 33.

9. A.W. Tozer, *The Knowledge of the Holy* (New York: HarperCollins Publishers, 1961), 1–2.

10. My thanks to Cathy Herndon, friend and Bible teacher at Heritage Baptist Church, Oklahoma City, for her suggestions and creative ideas on studying God's attributes and making a journal of reflections about God.

CHAPTER SIX: STEPPING INTO GOD'S PRESENCE

1. Richard Foster, *Prayer* (San Francisco: HarperSanFrancisco, 1992), 8–9.

2. A. W. Tozer, compiled by Warren W. Wiersbe, *The Best of A.W. Tozer* (Camp Hill, PA: Christian Publications, 1978), 221.

3. R. A. Torrey, *Prayer Portions for Daily Living* (Chicago: Moody Press, 1978), 311.

4. Eugene Peterson, *Answering God* (San Francisco: Harper & Row Publishers, 1989), 3–4.

5. Jill Harris adapted the "Prayer Sandwich" from Spiritual Formation Ministries, Nyack, NY.

6. From Jill Harris's children's prayer presentation, "M&M Kids." For information write P. O. Box 3929, Peachtree City, GA 30269 or call (770) 631-9900.

CHAPTER SEVEN: FROM WONDER TO WORSHIP

1. Evelyn Underhill, *The Love of God* (New York: Morehouse-Barlow Company, 1976), 134.

2. William Wordsworth, "Ode: Intimations of Immortality from Recollections of Early Childhood" in *The Oxford Book of English Verse* (Oxford: Clarendon Press, 1907), 611.

3. Alan D. Wright, *A Chance at Childhood Again* (Sisters, OR: Multnomah Publishers, 1997), 98.

4. Ibid., 103,

5. William Wordsworth, "The Rainbow," *The Oxford Book of English Verse,* 607.

6. Rabbi Marc Gellman and Monsignor Thomas Hartman, *How Do You Spell God?* (New York: Morrow Junior Books, 1995), 148–149.

7. Charles Spurgeon in *Prayer Portions for Daily Living* (Chicago: Moody Press, 1978), 121.

CHAPTER EIGHT: BEYOND THE CLATTERING CULTURE

1. Samuel Chadwick in *A Treasury of Prayer*, compiled by Leonard Ravenhill (Minneapolis: Bethany House Publishers, 1961), 186.

2. Geoffrey Cowley, *Newsweek* (March 6, 1995), 56.

3. Henri Nouwen, *Seeds of Hope* (New York: Bantam Books, 1989), 64.

4. Henri Nouwen, *Reaching Out* (New York: The Seabury Press, 1981), 136.

5. Brother Lawrence, *The Practice of the Presence of God* (Springdale, PA: Whitaker House), 1982.

6. Mother Teresa: *In My Own Words* (Ligouri, MO: Ligouri Publications, 1996), 7.

7. My thanks to Jill Harris for sharing this "Bouncing Ball" method to help children quiet their hearts for prayer.

8. David Wilkerson, "The Conspiracy of Interruptions," *Times Square Church Pulpit Series* (August 1997), 2–3.

CHAPTER NINE: THE JOY OF SERVANT PRAYERS

1. Karyn Henley, *Child-Sensitive Teaching* (Cincinnati: Standard Publishing, 1997), 38, 40.
2. Jill Johnstone, *You Can Change the World* (Grand Rapids: The Zondervan Corporation, 1992).
3. *Global Prayer Digest* a family devotional booklet published by the U. S. Center for World Missions, Pasadena, CA.
4. Patrick Johnstone, *Operation World* (Grand Rapids: The Zondervan Corporation, 1993).
5. Viva Network, Worldwide Day of Prayer for Children at Risk information packet. See Recommended Resources for more information.
6. Pete Hohmann, *The Great Commissionary Kids Intensive Care Unit: Mobilizing Kids for Outreach* (Springfield, MO: Boys and Girls Missionary Crusade, 1997), 37–38.
7. *Children's 30-Day Muslim Prayer Guide* (Colorado Springs: World Christian News, 1998).

CHAPTER TEN: THE POWER OF GOD'S PROMISES

1. Pete Hohmann, *The Great Commissionary Kids Intensive Care Unit: Mobilizing Kids for Outreach* (Springfield, MO: Boys and Girls Missionary Crusade, 1997), 12.
2. Judson Cornwall, *Praying the Scriptures* (Lake Mary, FL: Creation House, 1988), 75, 79.
3. Quin Sherrer, *How to Pray for Your Family and Friends* (Ann Arbor: Vine Books, 1990), 62.
4. My thanks to Joyce Satter, former King's Kids leader in Oregon, for her actual "checks" she distributes to explain the concept of likening God's Word to a two-party check.
5. Catherine Marshall, *Adventures in Prayer* (New York: Ballantine, 1975), 107.

CHAPTER ELEVEN: DIFFERENT KIDS, DIFFERENT BENTS

1. Alice Smith, "Praying Together: Annoying or Anointed?" *Pray!* Issue 6 (1998), 32–34.
2. W. H. P. Faunce in *Prayer Portions for Daily Living* (Chicago: Moody Press, 1978), 9.
3. Samuel Coleridge in John Bartlett, *Familiar Quotations* (Boston: Little, Brown, and Company, 1980), 435.

CHAPTER TWELVE: THE FAMILY THAT PRAYS TOGETHER

1. Eudora Welty, *One Writer's Beginnings* (New York: Warner Books, 1983), 10.
2. Paul Moede, "Here I Raise My What…?" *Discipleship Journal.* Issue 88 (1995), 90–2.

CHAPTER THIRTEEN: SMALL GROUPS, BIG ANSWERS

1. Fern Nichols, Moms In Touch International (Poway, CA: Moms In Touch International, 1987), 12.
2. Ibid., 12.
3. Julie Brown, *Kids Pray Resource Handbook* (Flagstaff, AZ: AmeriTribes, 1997).
4. Joyce and Paul Satter, *King's Kids Power in Prayer Intercession* (Salem, OR: P & J Satter, 1995), 3.

CHAPTER FOURTEEN: PRAYING KIDS ON CAMPUS

1. *National Network of Youth Ministries,* Volume 15, Number 3 (November 1997), 6.
2. Clarence P. Shedd, *Two Centuries of Student Christian Movements* (New York: Association Press, 1934), 1.
3. Timothy Beougher and Lyle Dorsett, editors, *Accounts of a Campus Revival* (Wheaton: Harold Shaw Publishers, 1995), 31–46.
4. To read more about the revival and youth prayer at Beech High School in Hendersonville, TN, reference my book *When Mothers Pray* (Sisters, OR: Multnomah Publishers, 1997).

CHAPTER FIFTEEN: PRAYERS HEARD 'ROUND THE WORLD

1. Lin Story, "The 1997 National Children's Prayer Congress," P. O. Box 9683, Washington, D.C., 20016.
2. Lin Story, *The Prayer Times,* Volume 1, No. 1 (1996), Washington, D.C., 6.

CHAPTER SIXTEEN: PREPARING FOR THE BATTLE

1. Jennifer Dean, *The Praying Life* (Birmingham, AL: New Hope, 1993), 32.
2. Wesley Duewel, *Mighty Prevailing Prayer* (Grand Rapids: Zondervan, 1990), 65.
3. Dean, 93.
4. Adapted from the Focus on the Family radio broadcast, "Community in Crisis" (December 1997), tape number BR253/20313, side 1.
5. Ken Walker, "The Day We Heard Gunfire," *Charisma & Christian Life* (March 1998), 78.
6. Tom White, "Families Under Attack," *Pray!* Issue 5 (1998), 17.

CHAPTER SEVENTEEN: OPENING UP THE PRAYER CLOSET

1. My thanks to Fawn Parish for contributing her insights and creativity as we brainstormed ways to integrate children into adult prayer sessions.

ABOUT THE AUTHOR

Cheri Fuller is a dynamic, inspirational speaker and author of numerous books on issues relating to children, women, the family, and learning. Cheri has a passion for prayer. As a leader of a local College Moms in Touch group, she experiences the power of prayer in her own life and the lives of other women. She also works with children in her church.

Cheri is a contributing editor for *Today's Christian Woman* and her articles regularly appear in *Focus on the Family, ParentLife, Family Circle,* and other magazines.

Cheri has been a frequent guest on *Focus on the Family,* Moody Network's *Midday Connection* and *Open Line,* and hundreds of radio stations across the country. A former teacher, she loves inspiring others as she speaks at women's retreats and conferences. Cheri and her husband, Holmes, have three grown children and live in Oklahoma City, Oklahoma.

If you have a creative idea or story about your family praying together or how God answered your prayers for your children or if you would like to contact Cheri for speaking engagements, write her at:

P.O. Box 770493
Oklahoma City, OK 73177
Fax: (405)749-1381
E-mail: 201-0444@mcimail.com